j.l.norton@icloud.com

© J L Norton 2024

GHOSTS BETWEEN US

Portsmouth, Present Day 1

Bournemouth Childhood 9

Senior School, First Cracks of Bullying 15

Beneath the Surface 27

Matthew Arrives 35

A Love in Bloom 43

Brave New World 51

Shadows of the Night 61

The Fall 69

Lost 77

Fury in the Silence 83

New Beginnings 89

Healing in the Fire 97

Unsettling Clues 103

Suspicions Grow 111

The Confession 119

Justice at Last 127

The Road Ahead 135

Chapter 1
PORTSMOUTH, PRESENT DAY

It had been a typical university social event—loud music, cheap drinks, and a crowded room filled with people Simon barely knew. He hadn't really wanted to go. Nights like this usually reminded him of the parts of himself he still wasn't sure he was ready to share. But his friends had dragged him along, promising it would be fun, and he had reluctantly agreed, telling himself that it couldn't hurt to at least try.

The bar was packed, the sound of laughter and clinking glasses blending with the bass-heavy music. Simon stood near the edge of the room, watching the mingling groups from a distance, a half-empty drink in his hand. He wore a dark, long-sleeved T-shirt that clung to his lean frame, paired with fitted black jeans and his usual worn-out Converse trainers. The shirt was simple and understated, something he felt comfortable in—nothing too attention-grabbing, just enough to blend in. He preferred it that way.

His friends were somewhere in the throng, but he felt disconnected from the noise, from the forced socialising. He wasn't sure how long he'd stay.

And then, in the midst of the chaos, he saw Andrew.

At first, it was nothing more than a brief glance—a casual scan of the room that landed on a face Simon hadn't seen before. Andrew was talking with a small group near the bar, his laugh carrying over the noise, his smile wide and easy. He was dressed in a form-fitting black T-shirt that hugged his chest and arms, showcasing the toned muscles beneath. His ripped jeans, with slashes across the knees and thighs, revealed glimpses of tanned skin, adding a casual yet rugged edge to his look. There was something effortlessly confident about him—like he belonged there, in that room, in that moment.

Simon's eyes flicked back to his drink, and he told himself it was nothing. Just another face in the crowd.

But a few moments later, Andrew was standing beside him, drink in hand, his smile as warm and genuine up close as it had been from across the room.

"Not really your scene, huh?" Andrew asked, his voice cutting through the noise with surprising ease.

Simon blinked, caught off guard by the sudden attention. "Uh, yeah," he replied, glancing around. "How'd you guess?"

Andrew shrugged, taking a sip of his drink. "You've got that 'I'd rather be anywhere else' look about you."

Simon chuckled softly, a little surprised at how quickly the tension in his chest eased. "I thought I was hiding it better."

"Nah," Andrew said, grinning. "But don't worry, I'm with you. These things are always a bit much. I came for the cheap drinks, stayed because… well, I don't know why I stayed."

There was something about Andrew's openness, the way he wasn't forcing the conversation, that made Simon relax. He felt the familiar urge to put up his guard, to deflect or withdraw, but Andrew wasn't pushing. He was just… there.

"I'm Simon, by the way," Simon said, holding out his hand.

"Andrew," he replied, shaking Simon's hand with an easy smile. "So, what do you study?"

They fell into conversation easily after that, the usual university small talk flowing between them with surprising fluidity. Simon found himself laughing more than he had expected, the tension in his chest gradually dissolving as they talked about everything from coursework to the local pubs in Portsmouth.

There was something different about Andrew. It wasn't just that he was easy to talk to–there was a warmth to him, a patience that Simon hadn't felt from anyone else in a long time. Andrew wasn't demanding his attention or prying into parts of Simon's life that he wasn't ready to share. He was just interested–genuinely interested– in what Simon had to say. It was refreshing. For the first time in what felt like years, Simon didn't feel like he was performing, like he had to keep up some sort of front.

The night passed quickly, and by the time the bar began to empty out, Simon was surprised to realise that he didn't want it to end.

"You want to grab coffee sometime?" Andrew asked casually as they headed toward the exit, his tone so light and unpressured that it almost caught Simon off guard.

Simon hesitated for only a second before nodding. "Yeah. I'd like that."

Their first coffee date was a few days later at a small café just off the main campus, a cosy place with soft lighting and worn leather chairs. It was quieter than the bar, the air filled with the comforting scent of brewing coffee and the low hum of conversation. Simon felt more at ease here, away from the noise and chaos of the university social scene.

Andrew was already seated when Simon arrived, a steaming cup of coffee in front of him and a book open on the table. He looked up as Simon approached, that same easy smile spreading across his face.

"Hey," Andrew said, closing the book and gesturing for Simon to sit. "I wasn't sure what you drank, so I didn't order for you."

Simon smiled as he sat down, appreciating the thoughtfulness. "No worries. I'll just get something quick."

After ordering, Simon returned to the table, settling into the comfortable chair across from Andrew. There was a slight awkwardness at first, the kind that comes with a second meeting, when the novelty of the initial conversation has worn off. But Andrew didn't seem fazed by it. He sipped his coffee, his gaze calm and attentive, waiting for Simon to start wherever he felt comfortable.

"So," Simon began, swirling the foam of his latte with a spoon, "you never told me what you're studying."

"History," Andrew said with a small laugh. "I know, pretty cliché. But I love it. I get to spend my time with old books and stories about people who screwed up in ways that somehow feel familiar, even though they lived centuries ago."

Simon grinned. "That's not cliché. That's interesting."

Andrew raised an eyebrow. "Oh yeah? And what's your passion?"

Simon hesitated, then shrugged. "English Lit. So I guess I'm not too far off. I spend my days reading about people who screw up, too –only in fiction."

They both laughed, and the tension between them dissolved completely. The conversation flowed more easily this time, their shared love of literature and history forming the foundation of their connection. They talked about their favourite authors, debated which historical figure had the most tragic story, and somehow, the hours slipped away.

Simon found himself lowering his guard, slowly but surely. It wasn't that he wanted to let someone in–part of him still resisted that–but with Andrew, it felt… safe. There was no pressure. Andrew wasn't prying into the parts of Simon's life that he wasn't ready to share. He wasn't pushing for more than Simon was willing to give. And that, more than anything, made Simon feel like maybe–just maybe–he could trust this.

They began meeting more regularly after that. Coffee dates turned into lunch breaks between lectures, which turned into evenings spent grabbing drinks at the pub, talking about everything from their course loads to their lives outside of university. Simon found himself thinking about Andrew more and more, looking forward to the time they spent together, feeling a quiet sense of excitement that he hadn't felt in years.

It wasn't just the chemistry between them—though that was undeniable, simmering just beneath the surface, waiting to be acknowledged. It was the way Andrew made Simon feel seen, the way he listened without judgement, laughed easily, and never pushed too hard. There was no expectation, no rush to define what was happening between them. And that, for Simon, was everything.

The first time they met for drinks in town, Simon noticed how easily Andrew fit into his world. They debated which pub in Portsmouth had the best atmosphere—Andrew leaning toward a lively place with loud music and a bustling crowd, while Simon preferred somewhere quieter, more intimate. They ended up compromising on a small bar tucked away in the city centre, where the music was soft enough for conversation but the atmosphere still buzzing with energy.

As they sipped their drinks, Simon found himself watching Andrew more closely, noticing the way his eyes crinkled when he laughed, the way he leaned in slightly when he was truly engaged in what Simon was saying. There was something about him that felt... promising. Maybe it was the way Andrew seemed genuinely interested in Simon's life—his past, his passions, the parts of him that Simon usually kept hidden. Or maybe it was the way Andrew could make him laugh, even on the days when Simon felt like retreating into himself.

For the first time since Matthew, Simon felt like he might be ready to try again. To let someone in. To believe that there was still room in his life for love.

And with Andrew, it felt like it could be something real.

Weeks turned into months, and their relationship grew. There were still moments when Simon's old fears crept in—moments when he would pull back, cautious, unsure of how much of himself he was ready to give. But Andrew never pushed. He never demanded more than Simon was willing to offer, and that patience, that quiet understanding, made Simon feel safe in a way he hadn't in years.

Simon wasn't sure where it was all heading, but for the first time in a long time, he wasn't afraid to find out.

Chapter 2
BOURNEMOUTH CHILDHOOD

Bournemouth had been Simon's whole world as a child with its picturesque coastline and leafy suburban streets. The air always smelled faintly of the sea, salty and crisp, a constant reminder that the beach was never far away. His early years were filled with moments of carefree joy–running through the sand, cycling through the quiet streets with his friends, and spending long afternoons at the park. But behind the innocent façade of his childhood, a quiet, growing confusion was taking root inside him, one that he didn't yet have the words to explain.

It started when Simon was ten. He didn't know exactly when or why, but he began to notice that he was different. At first, it was subtle–an extra glance at a boy who caught his eye, a flutter of something unfamiliar whenever he saw one of the older boys at school. It wasn't like anything he'd ever felt before. And it wasn't anything his friends seemed to experience.

Simon didn't understand it at first. He told himself that it was normal to admire his friends, to think about how cool or good-looking they were. But as the days passed, those feelings became something more—something he couldn't ignore. His friends were starting to talk about girls, laughing about who was the prettiest or who they fancied, but Simon felt none of it. Girls were just... there. They didn't stir anything inside him. But boys—boys were different.

He remembered one afternoon after football practice, sitting in the changing room with the other boys. The air was thick with the scent of sweat and the clatter of cleats being kicked off onto the floor. Simon sat on the bench, peeling off his socks, when he glanced up and saw one of the boys, Jamie, pulling off his shirt. Jamie's skin was flushed from running, his chest rising and falling as he caught his breath. Simon's gaze lingered a moment too long on the curve of Jamie's shoulders, the way his muscles moved beneath his skin, and an unexpected warmth spread through Simon's chest.

He quickly looked away, his heart hammering in his chest. What is this? he thought, his mind racing. He didn't have the words for it yet, but he knew that whatever he was feeling, it wasn't something he could talk about. Not with his friends, not with anyone.

The confusion gnawed at him, growing stronger as time went on. In class, he found his eyes wandering toward certain boys—wondering what it would be like to stand closer to them, to brush against them by accident, to feel their skin against his. He didn't fully understand why these thoughts came to him, only that they filled him with a strange mixture of excitement and fear. He'd look at boys like Ryan or Luke, who always seemed so effortlessly confident, and feel an overwhelming pull—like something was drawing him toward them, but at the same time, keeping him firmly at a distance.

There was something untouchable about them, these boys who seemed so close and yet impossibly far. They were like forbidden fruit–there to be admired but never reached. Simon could watch them, he could think about them in the quiet of his own mind, but he couldn't touch. He couldn't want them. Not openly, not safely.

The fear of being discovered was always there, lurking just beneath the surface of his thoughts. He had heard the way some of the other boys talked–their cruel jokes, their mocking laughter whenever someone dared to suggest that another boy was "different." Simon knew what they meant, and even though they never looked at him when they said those things, he felt exposed, like at any moment they might turn on him and realise the truth he was trying so hard to hide.

It wasn't just fear that kept him silent, though. There was something deeper, something more confusing. He didn't know how to be the way he felt. He didn't know what it would mean to act on these feelings, to reach out for the boys he found so compelling. They were beautiful to him in ways that stirred something deep inside, but they were also distant, out of reach. He wasn't ready to understand what he wanted, let alone take a step toward it.

In the privacy of his room, Simon would lie awake at night, staring at the ceiling, replaying moments from the day–moments when he had caught a glimpse of a boy's bare chest as he changed for PE, or when a friend had playfully nudged him, their arms brushing together. Those small, seemingly insignificant moments became the centre of Simon's thoughts. He'd feel a deep, aching need for something more, something he didn't have a name for, and it frightened him as much as it intrigued him.

The idea of acting on those feelings, of touching another boy the way his mind whispered to him in the quiet of the night, felt impossible. It wasn't just the fear of what others might think—it was the fear of what it would mean for him. He didn't understand what he was feeling, and without understanding, he couldn't make sense of it. All he knew was that the boys around him made his heart race in ways that girls never did.

Simon tried to push the thoughts away, tried to convince himself that they didn't matter. He threw himself into school, into his friendships, hoping that if he ignored the feelings, they would disappear. But they didn't. They only grew stronger, more insistent. Whenever he found himself alone with his thoughts, the images of boys would flood his mind—the curve of their backs as they leaned over their desks in class, the way their eyes sparkled when they laughed, the casual way they slung their arms around each other without a second thought. These were the things that filled Simon's mind, even though he knew he wasn't supposed to want them.

There were moments when he thought he might explode from the weight of it all—the longing, the confusion, the guilt. He would sit in class, pretending to listen to the teacher, while his mind wandered to places he couldn't speak about. He would sit next to a friend, their knee brushing against his under the desk, and he would feel like he was on fire, desperate for something he didn't know how to ask for.

But Simon was good at pretending. He had to be. So he kept it all inside, letting his fantasies and feelings swirl beneath the surface, always out of reach, always something he could think about but never act on. The boys were untouchable, just like the dreams he had of them—beautiful, fleeting, and distant.

And so Simon's childhood became a quiet struggle, a battle between what he felt and what he knew he couldn't have. He was only ten, but even then, he understood that what he wanted–what he was–was something that set him apart from the world around him. He didn't know what that meant for his future, but he knew that for now, it was something he had to keep hidden.

The boys remained his secret, his quiet obsession, the thing that made him feel alive in ways he couldn't explain. But they were also the thing he couldn't have, the path he didn't know how to take.

Chapter 3
SENIOR SCHOOL, FIRST CRACKS OF BULLYING

Starting senior school was supposed to feel like a new beginning. A fresh chapter in Simon's life. The sprawling red-brick building of the school loomed ahead as he walked through the gates on his first day, his heart pounding with nervous excitement. At eleven, Simon felt the mixture of fear and hope that most kids felt when starting a new school—hoping to fit in, fearing the unknown, and wondering where he would fall in the vast social hierarchy that dictated the lives of students.

He'd heard plenty of stories from older kids about how senior school was different—bigger, tougher. Friendships would change, cliques would form, and there would be new challenges. But there was another layer to Simon's nerves that none of his friends seemed to share. It wasn't just about making new friends or fitting in with the right crowd. Simon was also afraid of being noticed. Really noticed. For years now, he had quietly carried the weight of his secret, the gnawing realisation that he was different from the other boys. That he wasn't interested in girls the way they were. And the thought of anyone discovering that terrified him.

He kept his head down as he walked through the corridors on that first day, his new uniform crisp and uncomfortable. Boys jostled past him, laughing and shouting, their voices filling the space as they navigated their way to their classrooms. Simon tried to blend in, offering shy smiles to the boys from his old school who greeted him with a nod. But even then, in the chaotic energy of the first day, Simon could feel the weight of his own difference pressing down on him.

The first few weeks were manageable. Simon settled into a small group of friends, boys he'd known from primary school, and they stuck together, navigating the maze of new teachers, subjects, and the daunting presence of older students. But even in those early days, Simon was aware of the growing pressure to conform. The boys in his year were beginning to develop new interests, new ways of interacting with each other, and it didn't take long for Simon to realise that he was once again on the outside, looking in.

It started with the way they talked about girls.

By Year 8, the boys were already well into their routines of talking about girls–who was the prettiest, who had the best smile, who they fancied. They'd sit in groups at lunchtime, making crude jokes and rating the girls in their year with the kind of casual cruelty that only thirteen-year-old boys seemed capable of. Simon would sit quietly, pretending to go along with it, nodding when necessary, laughing when it seemed appropriate, but never offering any opinions of his own.

He'd learned early on how to play the game—how to pretend that he was just like them. When his friend Jack would elbow him and whisper, "You fancy any of the girls yet, Simon?" he'd force a grin and shrug. "Not really," he'd say, keeping his voice as neutral as possible. "Haven't thought about it."

It wasn't entirely a lie. He hadn't thought about the girls. He was too busy thinking about the boys.

Simon had tried, in those early months, to push those feelings down, to bury them deep inside himself where they couldn't be seen. He'd convinced himself that if he just ignored the way his heart raced whenever certain boys smiled at him or the way his gaze lingered just a bit too long in the changing room after PE, he could make it through school without anyone knowing.

But that was easier said than done.

By the time he was thirteen, Simon had developed his first real crush—an intense, overwhelming feeling that he had no idea how to handle. His crush was on Liam, a boy from his maths class. Liam had dark, messy hair and a cheeky grin that seemed to light up the room whenever he walked in. He was popular, always surrounded by friends, and completely oblivious to Simon's growing fascination with him.

Simon found himself watching Liam whenever they were in the same room, stealing glances at him during lessons, his heart pounding in his chest whenever Liam smiled or laughed. It was innocent, really–just the way Liam's eyes crinkled when he laughed, the casual way he slung his backpack over one shoulder, the way his voice sounded when he joked around with his friends. But it was enough to send Simon's mind spinning with feelings he didn't know how to control.

It didn't take long for the cracks to start showing.

Simon was quiet, sensitive, and not particularly interested in the rough-and-tumble nature of football or the bravado that seemed to come so easily to the other boys in his year. He preferred reading or drawing, losing himself in stories rather than joining in the constant banter and competition that defined most of the boys' interactions. He was different, and in a school full of boys desperate to assert their dominance and prove their masculinity, being different made him a target.

The first comment came in the middle of a PE lesson.

They were in the changing rooms, getting ready for a game of rugby, when one of the boys, Tom, made a snide remark. "Oi, Simon," Tom called across the room, his voice dripping with mockery. "Why are you always so quiet, mate? You fancy someone in here or what?"

The other boys snickered, and Simon's face flushed red. He didn't know how to respond. His mouth went dry, his heart racing as panic surged through him. He forced a laugh, shaking his head, but his silence only seemed to encourage them.

"Bet he fancies Liam," Tom sneered, glancing over at Simon with a smirk. "Always staring at him in maths, ain't you, Simon?"

Simon's stomach twisted. He hadn't thought anyone had noticed. He kept his head down, his fingers fumbling as he tied his rugby boots, willing himself to disappear. But the boys kept laughing, the sound echoing through the changing room, and Simon felt the first crack of fear splinter through him.

It didn't stop there. Once the boys had sensed that Simon was different, that there was something about him that didn't quite fit, they latched onto it like wolves scenting blood. The comments became more frequent–small jabs during lessons, whispered insults in the corridors, mocking laughs whenever Simon hesitated or stumbled.

"Oi, Simon, why don't you ever talk about girls, mate? What, you gay or something?"

The word gay was always spat out like a slur, something ugly and shameful. Simon would force a laugh, shake his head, and pretend it didn't bother him, but inside, it felt like a dagger twisting in his chest. He couldn't let them see how much it hurt. He couldn't let them know that they were right.

He wasn't out. He wasn't even fully sure what being "out" would look like. But the boys seemed to sense it anyway, that there was something about Simon that made him different from them. It was as if they could smell his fear, the way he tried so hard to blend in, to hide the truth about himself, and they used it against him.

The worst part was that Simon couldn't talk to anyone about it. He didn't have the words to explain what he was going through, and even if he did, he wasn't sure anyone would understand. His friends didn't seem to notice the bullying, or if they did, they didn't say anything. It was easier to pretend that it wasn't happening, that Simon wasn't slowly being pushed to the edges of their group, left to fend for himself as the insults and jabs became more frequent.

By the time he was fourteen, Simon had learned to keep his head down, to avoid drawing attention to himself. He tried to stay out of the way, hoping that if he didn't make a fuss, the boys would get bored and move on. But it wasn't that simple. The bullying wasn't always overt–sometimes it was as subtle as the way they'd look at him when he walked into a room, the way their laughter would stop when he passed by, only to start up again once he was out of earshot. Other times, it was more direct–an elbow to the ribs in the corridor, a whispered insult as they passed by, a shove that sent his books scattering across the floor.

It wore him down, slowly but surely. The constant pressure to fit in, to pretend he was something he wasn't, weighed on him like a heavy cloak. He wanted so badly to be like the other boys, to laugh with them, to join in their jokes without feeling like an outsider. But every time he tried, it felt wrong, like he was betraying himself.

The crushes didn't help. They came and went, intense and fleeting, leaving Simon feeling more confused than ever. There was Jamie, with his tousled hair and easy smile, who Simon spent too much time thinking about during lessons. Then there was Aaron, who sat next to Simon in geography, always leaning in close to whisper jokes about their teacher, his arm brushing against Simon's just enough to send a shiver down his spine. But no matter how much Simon liked them, no matter how much he fantasised about what it would be like to be close to them, he knew it was impossible.

They were boys. And boys weren't supposed to like other boys. At least, not in the way Simon did.

So Simon buried those feelings, shoving them down as deep as he could, hoping that if he ignored them, they would go away. But they didn't. They surfaced in the quiet moments, when Simon was alone in his room, lying in bed and thinking about the way Liam's hand had brushed his when they passed a ball ...when they passed a ball during PE. The memory of Liam's touch lingered in Simon's mind long after it had happened, and no matter how hard he tried, he couldn't shake it. It was so simple, so fleeting, yet it ignited something in him that he couldn't explain. It left him with a dull ache, a longing he had no way to express.

But it wasn't just Liam. Simon's feelings for boys surfaced in so many small ways–every time he caught a glimpse of one of his classmates changing in the locker room or when he watched the older boys at school play football during lunch. The sight of their muscular legs, the way their shirts clung to their bodies after practice, their carefree laughter as they wrestled or playfully shoved each other–it all stirred something deep inside him. But it was a desire he had no idea how to act on, a path that felt not just forbidden, but impossible.

The fear that someone would discover his secret grew alongside those feelings. He knew that the boys who mocked him for being quiet, for not joining in their crude jokes about girls, had already begun to suspect. It was in the way they looked at him, the way they called him names like "poof" and "fairy," words Simon barely understood but knew were meant to hurt. He could see it in their eyes–the way they probed, waiting for him to slip up, waiting for confirmation of what they thought they already knew.

Simon kept his guard up, building walls around himself, even as he longed for connection. He wished, sometimes desperately, that he could talk to someone–anyone–about what he was feeling. But there was no one. His parents, though loving, were traditional, and Simon couldn't imagine starting that conversation with them. His friends, though kind, were still boys, part of the same culture that demanded conformity and strength. The fear of being ostracised, of being left completely alone, kept Simon silent.

And so, Simon's world became smaller. He moved through the halls of the school like a ghost, careful to avoid the groups of boys who had started to become more aggressive in their teasing. He still hung out with his old friends, but even with them, there was a growing distance. He laughed when he needed to, smiled when expected, but inside, he felt like he was shrinking, retreating further and further into himself. He was desperate to keep his secret hidden, even as it threatened to consume him.

The bullying only got worse as the months wore on. The boys who had once been his friends now took every opportunity to make Simon feel small, to remind him that he didn't belong. They called him names, pushed him in the corridors, knocked his books from his hands. It was relentless, and though Simon tried to act like it didn't affect him, each insult cut deeper than the last.

There was one afternoon, in the changing rooms after football practice, that Simon would never forget. He was sitting on the bench, changing out of his kit, when he overheard a group of boys snickering in the corner. Tom, the ringleader, leaned against the wall, smirking as he looked over at Simon.

"Oi, Simon," Tom called, loud enough for everyone to hear. "You ever gonna tell us who you fancy, mate? Or is it one of us?"

The other boys burst into laughter, and Simon's face burned red. He tried to ignore them, tried to focus on lacing up his trainers, but his hands were shaking, and his mind was racing. He didn't know what to say, how to defend himself. The fear of being exposed, of having his secret laid bare in front of everyone, paralysed him.

Tom stepped closer, his smirk widening as he sensed Simon's discomfort. "Come on, we all know you're into blokes, Simon. Just admit it."

Simon's throat tightened, and he could feel the stares of the other boys on him, waiting for his response. He wanted to shout, to tell them to leave him alone, but the words wouldn't come. Instead, he just stood there, frozen, his mind spinning with panic.

It was Liam, the boy Simon had been crushing on for months, who broke the silence.

"Leave him alone, Tom," Liam said, his voice firm but not unkind. "You're being a dick."

For a moment, Simon's heart soared. He looked up at Liam, gratitude flooding his chest. But the relief was short-lived. Tom just laughed, shrugging as he turned to Liam.

"Alright, alright," Tom said, holding up his hands in mock surrender. "Didn't know you were his protector. Maybe you fancy him, eh?"

Liam rolled his eyes, brushing off the comment, but Simon could see the flicker of discomfort in his expression. And that was enough. The dynamic in the room shifted, and Simon felt the hope he'd been clinging to slip through his fingers. Even Liam, as kind as he was, couldn't be associated with someone like Simon. It was too dangerous. Too risky.

The bullying didn't stop after that day. If anything, it intensified. But something had shifted inside Simon. The more the boys taunted him, the more he realised that there was no escaping who he was. He couldn't keep pretending forever. He couldn't keep hiding from himself.

Still, the idea of coming out, of letting the world know the truth about him, felt terrifying. He wasn't ready. Not yet. He didn't even know how to begin that conversation, and the fear of being rejected –by his friends, by his family, by everyone he cared about–kept him silent.

But even in the silence, even as the bullying continued and the pressure built, Simon knew that he couldn't suppress his feelings forever. He could try to push them down, to bury them deep inside, but they would always find a way to surface. Every crush, every lingering glance in the changing room, every whispered insult in the corridor–it was all part of a truth that Simon was slowly starting to accept.

He was gay.

And even though he wasn't ready to say it out loud, even though the path ahead was filled with uncertainty and fear, Simon knew that it was a part of him that couldn't be erased. It was who he was, and no amount of bullying or denial could change that.

For now, though, Simon would keep his head down, bide his time, and wait for the moment when he was ready to step into the light.

Chapter 4
BENEATH THE SURFACE

By the time Simon turned fifteen, he was fully aware of who he was, even if he wasn't ready to say it out loud. He was gay. He'd known it for years now, but the clarity of that truth hadn't brought him any closer to understanding what it meant. There were no guides, no role models he could turn to for advice. His only education on what it meant to be gay came from whispers in the corridors, bits of crude porn he found online late at night, and stolen glances at boys in the changing rooms. It was a world he felt he didn't belong to, but one he was desperate to understand.

He longed for connection—something that went beyond the furtive crushes and the hidden glances. But all Simon had ever known was that this part of himself was something to be kept secret, to be buried. And as the pressure to be someone he wasn't mounted, Simon's desperation to explore the parts of himself he had been suppressing only grew.

One night, after scrolling through social media, Simon stumbled across a gay dating app. He stared at it for a long time, his heart racing in his chest. He was alone in his room, the only sound the low hum of his laptop. His hands shook as he hesitated before downloading it. He had heard about these apps from whispers in the schoolyard, from older boys talking about hookups and "finding a quick one." But this was different. For Simon, it was an opening—a doorway to the world he'd been too afraid to explore.

It felt dangerous. Thrilling. But also terrifying.

His first encounters weren't the grand romantic moments he had imagined. They were messy, awkward, and, at times, painful in ways that he hadn't anticipated. The first time Simon met a boy from the app, his hands trembled as he stepped out of his house and headed toward the nearby park where they had arranged to meet. The boy, Josh, was a few years older, with an air of confidence that made Simon's stomach twist in both excitement and fear.

When Simon finally saw him, sitting on a bench, it felt surreal. Josh was handsome, undeniably so—tall with dark hair and piercing eyes. Simon felt his pulse quicken as he walked over, the reality of what he was doing sinking in. They exchanged a few nervous words, a shared laugh, before Josh suggested they go somewhere "quieter."

Simon followed him, his heart pounding in his ears.

They found a secluded corner near the edge of the park, hidden from view by a cluster of trees. Simon's mind raced, torn between wanting this, needing this, and the overwhelming fear of what was about to happen. Josh leaned in, his breath warm against Simon's skin as their lips met in a rushed, hungry kiss. For a moment, Simon's thoughts scattered, lost in the sensation of finally kissing another boy—something he had imagined for years but had never experienced.

But it wasn't how Simon had pictured it. The kiss was rough, urgent, lacking the tenderness Simon had hoped for. Josh's hands moved quickly, tugging at Simon's clothes, pulling him closer, and for a brief second, Simon felt like he was being swept away in a current he didn't know how to navigate. It was happening too fast. Too intense.

When it was over, Simon stood there, breathless, his heart still racing. Josh pulled away, adjusting his clothes, already looking distracted, distant. There was no lingering touch, no smile or shared glance of understanding. It felt transactional, like a brief encounter that had no real meaning beyond the physical act.

Simon left the park that night feeling hollow, confused, and strangely ashamed. He had wanted this—had wanted to explore what it meant to be gay, to be with a boy—but the reality of it left him feeling more isolated than ever. There had been no connection, no intimacy. Just the raw, awkward reality of two bodies coming together and then parting just as quickly.

Over the next few months, Simon found himself falling into a pattern. He continued meeting boys through the app, each encounter different but somehow the same. There were moments of excitement–of feeling alive in the rush of a kiss, in the heat of skin against skin–but those moments always faded, leaving behind a sense of emptiness that Simon couldn't shake. He would leave these encounters feeling more lost than before, the weight of what he was doing pressing down on him like a lead blanket.

The nights alone in his room became harder. After each encounter, Simon would lie in bed, staring at the ceiling, wondering what was wrong with him. Why wasn't this enough? Why wasn't the thrill of being with another boy satisfying the ache he felt deep inside? He had thought that these experiences would make him feel whole, but instead, they only deepened his sense of isolation. He felt more like an outsider now than he ever had before.

The confusion bled into his days. At school, Simon found it harder to concentrate, harder to keep up the façade of being just another normal boy. The bullying hadn't stopped–if anything, it had gotten worse. The whispers had turned into full-blown taunts. Words like "faggot" and "poof" followed him through the halls, accompanied by snickers and knowing glances.

"Oi, Simon," one of the boys would shout during break. "Got a boyfriend yet?"

The laughter that followed was sharp, cutting through Simon like a blade. He tried to ignore it, to keep his head down and pretend it didn't bother him, but the truth was, it was starting to wear him down. The relentless bullying, combined with the emptiness he felt after each encounter, left Simon feeling trapped. He didn't know how to be himself, but he also didn't know how to keep pretending.

And so, Simon began to spiral.

The excitement he had once felt about being with boys, about exploring his sexuality, started to turn into something darker. He began to dread the encounters, even as he craved them. Each time he met someone new, he would feel the familiar rush of anticipation, followed by the inevitable crash afterward. The cycle repeated itself, and with each new encounter, Simon felt himself slipping further and further away from who he was.

He couldn't talk to anyone about it. His parents wouldn't understand. His friends at school were oblivious, too caught up in their own lives to notice Simon's growing distance. And the boys he met on the app? They were strangers–temporary, fleeting moments of connection that disappeared as quickly as they arrived.

It wasn't long before Simon's mental health began to deteriorate. The confusion he felt about his identity, the shame that came with every failed encounter, and the relentless bullying all piled on top of each other, crushing him under their weight. He started to withdraw, not just from his friends, but from the world around him. He stopped participating in class, his grades began to slip, and he spent more and more time locked away in his room, trying to make sense of the chaos in his mind.

There were nights when Simon would lie awake, staring at the darkness, feeling like he was drowning. The loneliness was unbearable, a constant ache that gnawed at him from the inside. He thought about ending it sometimes, about what it would be like if the pain just… stopped. But even those thoughts felt distant, like they belonged to someone else.

He didn't know how to reach out for help. He didn't even know if help was something he deserved.

One night, after yet another brief and unsatisfying encounter, Simon sat on the edge of his bed, staring down at his hands. They were trembling, his body still buzzing from the adrenaline, but his mind was somewhere else–far away, lost in the dark fog that had settled over him. He felt hollow, like a shell of the person he used to be, and he didn't know how to fill the emptiness.

That night, for the first time, Simon allowed himself to cry. The tears came slowly at first, a quiet release of the pain he had been carrying for so long. But soon, they became something more–a flood of emotion that he couldn't hold back any longer. The sobs wracked his body, shaking him to his core as he curled up on his bed, letting the weight of everything he had been suppressing pour out of him.

The confusion. The shame. The fear. It all came crashing down on him, and for the first time, Simon let himself feel it.

He didn't know what the future held. He didn't know if he would ever find the connection he so desperately craved, or if the emptiness inside him would ever be filled. But in that moment, as he lay there in the darkness, Simon made a quiet promise to himself.

He wasn't ready to give up. Not yet.

Chapter 5
MATTHEW ARRIVES

Simon had grown used to the routine of sixth form—keeping his head down, blending into the background as much as possible. His small circle of friends had thinned out over the years, and while he still saw a few familiar faces in his classes, Simon often felt like a ghost, drifting through the corridors with no real connection to the world around him. The bullying had died down somewhat, but the loneliness remained, a constant weight that sat heavy in his chest.

He had become an expert at hiding his true self, at burying the parts of him that longed for something more—for connection, for love, for understanding. After years of confusion and painful encounters, Simon had all but resigned himself to the fact that he would always feel this way. Isolated. Unseen.

And then Matthew arrived.

It was a warm September morning when Simon first noticed him. He was standing in the courtyard, a new face among the familiar crowd of sixth-formers, leaning casually against one of the low brick walls that lined the perimeter of the school. There was something about him that immediately caught Simon's attention–a kind of quiet confidence, the way he stood as though he was entirely at ease with himself.

Matthew had dark, wavy hair that fell just over his eyes and a natural charm that seemed to radiate from him, even from a distance. He was talking with a group of boys, laughing at something one of them had said, but it wasn't the laughter that made Simon's heart skip. It was the way Matthew's eyes scanned the crowd, like he was looking for something–or someone.

For the rest of the day, Simon couldn't stop thinking about him. It was rare for someone new to join in the middle of sixth form, and even rarer for them to blend in so quickly. But Matthew wasn't like the others. There was an openness to him, a warmth that Simon hadn't seen in a long time, not in this school. He seemed... different.

It wasn't long before Simon and Matthew were in the same class together. English Literature. Simon had always loved the subject–it was one of the few things that made him feel alive, the way words on a page could take him to another world, far from the one that had always felt so suffocating. But sitting two rows in front of Matthew, Simon found it impossible to concentrate on anything except the boy with the easy smile and the dark, thoughtful eyes.

One afternoon, after class had ended, Simon lingered behind, packing his books into his bag as the other students filed out. As he zipped up his bag, he felt a presence beside him and looked up to see Matthew standing there, a relaxed smile on his face.

"Hey, you're Simon, right?"

Simon blinked, surprised that Matthew even knew his name. "Yeah," he replied, trying to keep his voice steady. "That's me."

Matthew grinned, shifting his weight from one foot to the other. "You're in my English class. I've seen you around, but we haven't really talked." He hesitated for a moment, then added, "I just transferred here a few weeks ago, so I'm still getting the hang of things."

Simon nodded, trying to ignore the fluttering in his chest. "Yeah, I noticed you were new. How are you finding it so far?"

"It's alright," Matthew said with a shrug. "Different from my last school, but in a good way, I think."

Simon wasn't sure what to say next, his mind racing as he tried to process the fact that Matthew was standing here, talking to him. He hadn't had many genuine conversations with boys his age—at least, not ones that felt easy, natural. But there was something about Matthew's presence that made Simon feel... seen.

"I'm heading to the library," Matthew said after a brief pause, glancing toward the door. "You coming? Could use some company."

Simon blinked, momentarily thrown by the invitation. He hadn't expected Matthew to ask him to hang out, and the suddenness of it made his heart skip a beat. But something in Matthew's tone, in the casual way he asked, put Simon at ease. It didn't feel like there were any expectations, no pressure–just an offer.

"Sure," Simon said, grabbing his bag. "I'll come."

As they walked to the library, their conversation flowed easily. Matthew asked Simon about his favourite books, and they spent the next half hour talking about literature, sharing their favourite stories, and laughing about the terrible books they'd been forced to read in school. For the first time in what felt like forever, Simon felt a sense of lightness–like he didn't have to pretend to be someone he wasn't. Matthew wasn't like the other boys. He didn't push or prod. He didn't ask the awkward, invasive questions Simon had grown used to. He just... talked. And listened.

Over the next few weeks, Simon and Matthew began to spend more time together. They'd sit next to each other in English, exchange glances during lessons, and meet up after school to grab coffee or just walk through the park, talking about everything and nothing. It was easy, effortless, and Simon quickly realised that he had never felt this kind of connection with anyone before. Not like this.

One afternoon, they found themselves sitting on a bench at the edge of the park, watching the leaves fall as autumn crept in. The air was cool, and the sun hung low in the sky, casting a soft golden light over everything. Matthew turned to Simon, his eyes serious but warm.

"You know," Matthew began, his voice soft, "I haven't really talked about this with anyone at school yet, but… I'm gay."

The words hung in the air between them, and for a moment, Simon didn't know how to respond. His heart was racing, his mind spinning. He had never heard someone say it so plainly, so confidently. Matthew wasn't ashamed, wasn't hiding. He was just… being himself.

Simon swallowed, his throat suddenly dry. "I am too," he whispered, the words slipping out before he had time to think about them.

Matthew smiled, a genuine, understanding smile that made Simon's chest tighten with emotion. "I kind of thought so," he said, his voice gentle. "I mean, I wasn't sure, but… I don't know. I had a feeling."

Simon felt like the ground had shifted beneath him. He had spent years hiding this part of himself, terrified of what it would mean if anyone found out. And yet here was Matthew, sitting next to him, smiling like it was the most natural thing in the world.

For the first time in his life, Simon didn't feel alone.

Their relationship blossomed after that. It started with stolen glances in class, quiet moments where their hands would brush against each other's under the table, sending a thrill through Simon's body. They didn't talk about it much at first–there was no need. It was there, unspoken, but understood. Something special had grown between them, something that went beyond friendship.

One evening, after they had spent the afternoon at Matthew's house, Simon found himself sitting on the edge of Matthew's bed, his heart pounding in his chest. They had been watching a film, but neither of them had paid much attention to it. The air between them felt charged, like something was about to happen.

Matthew shifted closer to Simon, his eyes searching Simon's face for any sign of hesitation. When Simon didn't pull away, Matthew leaned in, his breath warm against Simon's skin as he whispered, "Is this okay?"

Simon nodded, his voice caught in his throat. "Yeah," he whispered back, his heart racing.

Matthew kissed him then—soft and tentative at first, but quickly deepening as Simon kissed him back. It was everything Simon had imagined and more. There was none of the awkwardness or confusion that had accompanied his past encounters, none of the shame that had always lingered afterward. This was different. This was real.

They became inseparable after that. Their relationship was a secret—something they kept hidden from most of their peers. Simon wasn't ready to come out to the world, and Matthew respected that. But in the quiet moments they shared together, Simon felt like he was finally able to be himself, without fear, without judgement.

Matthew was his anchor, his beacon of hope in the middle of the storm that had been Simon's life for so long. For the first time, Simon felt like he wasn't alone in the world. He had Matthew. And that was enough.

But even amidst the joy of their growing relationship, there was still an undercurrent of fear. They kept their love hidden, careful not to draw attention to themselves at school. The world outside was still unforgiving, still filled with the same people who had taunted Simon for years. But with Matthew by his side, the weight of that fear felt a little lighter.

Simon had found something he hadn't even known he was looking for–a boy who saw him, understood him, and loved him for exactly who he was.

And in Matthew's arms, Simon began to believe that maybe, just maybe, things would be okay.

Chapter 6
A LOVE IN BLOOM

The autumn months passed in a blur of stolen moments and secret smiles, and Simon found himself feeling something he hadn't experienced in years–happiness. Real, bone-deep happiness. It was a feeling that had once seemed so distant, so impossible, but with Matthew by his side, everything felt different. For the first time in his life, Simon wasn't just surviving–he was living.

Their relationship deepened quickly. What had begun as shy glances and quiet conversations soon became something more. They grew closer with each passing day, finding new ways to be with each other, away from the eyes of their peers. Their world was a secret, one they had built together in the spaces where no one could judge or hurt them.

On weekends, they would escape to the beach, taking the bus down town to where the shoreline stretched for miles, dotted with small, secluded spots that felt like they belonged only to them. The cold wind whipped through their hair, and the crash of the waves was a constant backdrop to their whispered conversations. Simon would sit beside Matthew on the sand, their shoulders brushing as they looked out at the endless sea, and for a while, everything seemed simple.

Those beach getaways became their sanctuary. Simon loved the way the sunlight glinted off Matthew's dark hair, the way his smile lit up his whole face when he laughed. They would walk along the shore, hands brushing but never fully entwined in case someone saw. But when they were far enough away from the crowds, from anyone who might recognise them, Simon would take Matthew's hand in his, feeling the warmth and the quiet strength in his touch.

It was in those moments, the ones where it was just the two of them, that Simon felt most free.

They spent hours at the beach, talking about everything and nothing. Matthew had a way of drawing Simon out, of making him feel like he could say anything without fear of judgment. They talked about their favourite films, the future, and sometimes, in hushed tones, about what it was like to be gay in a world that didn't always make space for them.

"It's scary sometimes," Simon admitted one evening as they sat huddled together, the fading sunlight casting a golden glow over the sand. "I mean, being... this. Us."

Matthew nodded, his arm around Simon's shoulders, pulling him close. "I know. But it's worth it, right?"

Simon leaned into him, letting the weight of Matthew's arm anchor him. "Yeah. It's worth it."

Those beach days were their escape from the pressures of school and the fear of being found out. But they had other escapes too—ones that were riskier, but no less thrilling.

One night, Matthew leaned over the table at a quiet café, his eyes twinkling with mischief. "You ever been to a gay bar?"

Simon blinked, taken aback by the sudden question. "A gay bar? No. Why?"

Matthew grinned. "There's one in the Triangle. DYMK. The doorman's a friend of my older brother, so he might let us in. What do you think?"

The idea made Simon's stomach flip. The thought of going somewhere where he could be himself, where he wouldn't have to hide, was both terrifying and exhilarating. He had heard about DYMK from whispers around town, but it had always seemed like something out of reach, something for other people—not for someone like him.

But Matthew's grin was infectious, and the more Simon thought about it, the more he wanted to say yes. He could already picture it—the lights, the music, the freedom of being in a place where no one would care if he held Matthew's hand, if he kissed him in the middle of the dance floor.

"Alright," Simon said, a smile tugging at the corners of his mouth. "Let's do it."

The night they went to DYMK was one Simon would never forget.

They arrived at the Triangle just after ten, the streets already buzzing with the energy of a Saturday night. The bar stood out, its bright neon sign glowing against the dark sky. Simon's heart raced as they approached the entrance, a mix of nerves and excitement swirling in his chest.

The doorman, a tall guy with a friendly smile, nodded at Matthew as they approached. "Alright, mate," he said, his voice low and easy. "Your brother said you might be coming down. You're good to go in."

Matthew grinned, giving Simon a quick, excited glance before leading him inside.

The bar was everything Simon had imagined and more. The air was thick with the scent of sweat and alcohol, the music pulsing through the space in a steady rhythm. Bright lights flashed across the room, casting the crowd in hues of pink and blue, and everywhere Simon looked, there were men—dancing, laughing, holding each other close.

It was a world Simon had only dreamed about, and now, he was standing right in the middle of it.

Matthew led him to the bar, where they ordered drinks—something sweet and fruity that made Simon's head spin after just a few sips. They stood together, leaning against the bar as they took it all in. The crowd was mostly older than them—men in their twenties, thirties, even forties—but Simon didn't care. For the first time in his life, he felt like he was in a place where he belonged.

After a few drinks, Matthew tugged at Simon's hand, pulling him toward the dance floor. The music shifted to something upbeat and familiar—a cheesy pop track that Simon vaguely recognised—and soon they were in the thick of it, bodies moving all around them, the heat of the room pressing in.

Matthew, always more confident than Simon, was the first to peel off his shirt, tossing it to the side as he grinned at Simon. "Come on," he urged, his voice barely audible over the music. "Join me."

Simon hesitated for a moment, his eyes darting around the room. But then he saw the way Matthew was looking at him—eyes full of laughter and warmth—and any hesitation he had melted away. He pulled off his shirt, feeling the cool air against his skin, and suddenly, they were both laughing, arms around each other as they moved to the music.

They danced like that for what felt like hours, bodies pressed together, sweaty and breathless. Simon's head was spinning, not just from the alcohol but from the sheer joy of it all. He didn't care about the other men in the room, didn't care about the way some of them were watching. The only person that mattered was Matthew.

There was a moment, in the middle of it all, when Simon pulled Matthew closer, their bodies flush against each other. The lights flickered above them, casting shadows across Matthew's face, and for a brief second, it was just the two of them—no bar, no music, no crowd. Just Simon and Matthew, in their own little world.

"You're amazing," Simon whispered, his lips brushing against Matthew's ear.

Matthew smiled, his hands resting on Simon's hips. "So are you."

They kissed then, right there on the dance floor, surrounded by the thrum of the music and the heat of the crowd. It was reckless, maybe even a little dangerous, but Simon didn't care. For the first time in his life, he felt truly free—free to love, to be loved, without fear or shame.

As the night wore on, they continued to dance, lost in each other. The world outside the bar, with all its expectations and judgments, felt far away. In here, they were just two boys in love, dancing under the flashing lights, completely at ease in their own skin.

The months that followed were some of the best of Simon's life. His relationship with Matthew flourished, growing stronger with each passing day. They still kept their relationship a secret from most of their peers, careful not to draw too much attention to themselves at school. But in the moments when they were alone–whether at the beach, in Matthew's room, or on the dance floor at DYMK–Simon felt like he had found something he had always been searching for.

Matthew was his beacon of hope, his safe harbour in a world that had so often felt unwelcoming. And for the first time in his life, Simon allowed himself to believe that love–real, messy, beautiful love–was possible for someone like him.

They still had to navigate the challenges of growing up gay in a world that didn't always understand them. There were moments of fear, moments when the weight of their secret felt overwhelming. But with Matthew by his side, Simon felt stronger than he ever had before.

Their love, like the ocean they so often escaped to, was vast and untamed, full of possibility. And as long as they had each other, Simon knew that they could face whatever came next.

Chapter 7
BRAVE NEW WORLD

For Simon, Matthew had become more than just a boyfriend—he was everything. He was the embodiment of hope, the one person who saw Simon for who he truly was, without judgement or fear. Their relationship had deepened in ways Simon could never have imagined. The loneliness, the confusion, and the shame that had weighed on Simon for years now felt like distant memories, overshadowed by the love he had found in Matthew.

By the time they entered their final year of sixth form, Simon and Matthew were inseparable. They no longer cared what people at school thought or whispered about them. There was strength in their unity, and the more time they spent together, the more confident Simon became. Together, they walked the halls with their heads held high, hands brushing against each other in quiet moments, smiles exchanged that needed no words. The world around them might still have been filled with uncertainty, but as long as Simon had Matthew, none of it mattered.

Outside of school, their connection only grew stronger. They spent weekends in each other's company, whether that meant lazy mornings in bed at Matthew's house, exploring Bournemouth's hidden corners, or returning to the beach that had become their favourite escape. The beach was where Simon felt the most at peace. It was where they could be themselves, no eyes watching, no questions asked. It was just them, the endless sea, and the promise of something bigger than the small world they knew.

But as free as Simon felt with Matthew, there was still one last barrier he hadn't crossed: coming out to his parents.

It wasn't that he thought they would react badly–deep down, Simon knew his parents were loving, open-minded people. But that didn't make the conversation any less terrifying. Telling his friends at school, dealing with the occasional side-eye or snide remark, that had been easier with Matthew by his side. But coming out to his family felt different. It felt… final, like once the words were spoken, there would be no going back.

The fear of disappointing them, of not living up to the version of the son they had in their minds, weighed heavily on Simon. His parents had always been supportive, but there was something about the idea of telling his dad, especially, that made Simon's stomach twist with anxiety. Telling another man, a man who had raised him, that he wasn't the same kind of man–at least, not in the way his father might have expected–seemed impossible.

It was Matthew who encouraged him to take the leap.

"You'll feel better once it's out in the open," Matthew said one evening as they lay on Simon's bed, their fingers intertwined. "And I'll be right here, with you, no matter what."

Simon nodded, though the knot of fear still tightened in his chest. "I know... I just... What if it changes things?"

Matthew squeezed Simon's hand gently. "It won't. They love you. You're still their son, no matter what. And they've probably already figured it out."

Simon chuckled, though the nerves were still there. "Maybe."

The conversation weighed on Simon's mind for days, but Matthew was right—his parents deserved to know the truth, and Simon knew he couldn't hide who he was any longer. He had already spent too many years pretending to be something he wasn't. He didn't want to live in the shadows anymore.

One Sunday afternoon, Simon decided to tell his mum first. It wasn't that he thought she would take the news any better than his dad, but there was something about talking to her that felt a little easier. She had always been the more emotionally open of his parents, always ready to listen and offer a comforting word.

Simon found her in the kitchen, peeling potatoes for dinner, the smell of roast chicken filling the room. She smiled at him as he walked in, though her eyes were filled with the kind of quiet curiosity that told Simon she already sensed something was on his mind.

"Hey, love," she said, glancing up from the chopping board. "Everything alright?"

Simon swallowed, feeling his heart hammer in his chest. His palms were sweating, and for a moment, he thought about backing out, about putting it off just one more day. But then he thought of Matthew, of the way he had promised to be by Simon's side through all of this, and something inside Simon shifted. He couldn't keep hiding anymore.

"Mum," Simon began, his voice shaky but determined. "I need to tell you something."

His mum paused, turning to face him fully now, the smile fading into a look of concern. "What is it, Simon?"

Simon took a deep breath, forcing the words to come. "I… I'm gay."

The silence that followed was brief but felt like an eternity. His mum's eyes widened slightly, her hands still resting on the chopping board, but there was no shock or anger in her expression –just a quiet, thoughtful pause. And then, slowly, she smiled.

"Oh, Simon," she said softly, stepping toward him and wrapping him in a warm embrace. "I wondered if you might be. I'm so proud of you for telling me."

Simon felt his heart swell with relief, the tension in his body melting away as he buried his face in his mum's shoulder. The fear, the anxiety, it all seemed to dissolve in her arms.

"You're not disappointed?" Simon asked, his voice muffled.

"Of course not," his mum said, pulling back to look him in the eye. "You're still the same Simon you've always been. The same son we love. This doesn't change anything."

Simon felt a tear slip down his cheek, though it was more from the overwhelming relief than anything else. His mum wiped it away gently with her thumb, her smile still soft and reassuring.

"And Matthew?" she asked. "Is he the boy you've been spending all your time with?"

Simon nodded, his cheeks flushing slightly. "Yeah. He is."

His mum's smile widened. "I thought so. You've been talking about him non-stop for months."

Simon laughed, feeling lighter than he had in weeks. "I guess I have."

"I'm glad you've found someone who makes you happy," his mum said, reaching up to brush a stray lock of hair from his forehead. "We'll have to invite him over for dinner one of these days. Get to know him properly."

The thought of Matthew sitting at their dinner table, chatting with his parents like everything was normal, sent a warm rush through Simon's chest. It was the kind of acceptance he had never dared to hope for.

With his mum's support, telling his dad seemed a little less daunting. Later that evening, as they sat in the living room, Simon braced himself for another difficult conversation. His dad was reading the newspaper, his glasses perched on the end of his nose, looking every bit the man Simon had always known him to be– practical, reserved, but loving in his own quiet way.

"Dad," Simon said, his voice steady but nervous. "Can we talk?"

His dad lowered the newspaper, looking over at Simon with a curious frown. "Of course, son. What's on your mind?"

Simon took a deep breath, the familiar fear creeping back in, but he pushed through it. "I... I'm gay."

For a moment, his dad didn't say anything. He just looked at Simon, his face unreadable. The silence stretched on, and Simon felt his heart begin to race, wondering if this had been a mistake, if maybe this conversation wouldn't go as well as it had with his mum.

But then his dad sighed softly and nodded. "Alright," he said, his voice calm and measured. "Thank you for telling me."

Simon blinked, surprised by the simplicity of the response. "That's it?"

His dad smiled faintly, folding the newspaper and setting it aside. "That's it. You're still my son, Simon. That's never going to change. You're not any different today than you were yesterday."

Simon let out a breath he hadn't realised he'd been holding. His dad's acceptance wasn't as effusive as his mum's, but it was there, solid and unwavering.

"You're not disappointed?" Simon asked, the question slipping out before he could stop it.

His dad shook his head. "No, Simon. I'm not. You're a good lad. You've always been a good lad. Who you love doesn't change that."

Simon felt his chest swell with emotion, and for the first time in his life, he felt like he could truly breathe.

"Is Matthew, the one you've been spending all your time with, your boyfriend?" his dad asked, echoing his mum's earlier question.

Simon nodded, a small smile playing on his lips. "Yeah. He is."

His dad leaned back in his chair, a thoughtful expression on his face. "Seems like a good kid. You bring him round for dinner sometime, alright? We'd like to meet him."

Simon smiled, a feeling of peace settling over him. "Yeah. I'd like that."

The days that followed felt like a new chapter in Simon's life. With Matthew's love, and his parents' acceptance, Simon felt like he could do anything. There was no more hiding, no more fear of being discovered. He had his family's love, Matthew's support, and a future that suddenly seemed brighter than it ever had before.

For the first time, Simon believed that the world might just be a place where he could be himself–fully, without shame, without fear.

And with Matthew by his side, nothing could stop them.

Chapter 8
SHADOWS OF THE NIGHT

It had been a night like so many others before it—Simon and Matthew together, laughing, carefree, and utterly absorbed in each other's company. They had spent the evening at one of their favourite pubs, tucked away in a quiet corner of Bournemouth, just enjoying the simplicity of being together. The warmth of their love had felt unshakable, like nothing could penetrate the bubble they had created for themselves.

But as they left the pub that night, stepping out into the cool night air, the world around them felt different. It was subtle at first, a shift in the atmosphere that Simon barely registered. The streets were quieter than usual, the echo of their footsteps the only sound as they made their way down the dimly lit road. The distant hum of traffic seemed far away, and the sky was unusually dark, the moon hidden behind a blanket of thick clouds.

Simon glanced over at Matthew, his heart swelling with affection. They had been talking about their plans for the weekend, maybe another trip to the beach, but the details were lost in the warmth of their conversation. Matthew had his arm slung over Simon's shoulder, casual and confident, like he always did when they were out late. They no longer cared who saw them together, who might whisper behind their backs. They had each other, and that had always been enough.

But tonight, something felt off. Simon couldn't shake the feeling that they weren't as alone as they thought. He quickened his pace slightly, his eyes darting around the empty street.

"Everything alright?" Matthew asked, sensing Simon's unease.

Simon nodded, forcing a smile. "Yeah, just… feels quiet, that's all."

Matthew chuckled softly, pulling Simon a little closer. "It's late. I think the town's gone to bed."

But the feeling lingered. Simon's heart began to race, his body tense. As they rounded a corner, heading toward the quieter end of town where the shadows seemed to stretch further than they should, Simon heard it–footsteps. Behind them. Slow at first, almost in time with their own.

He glanced over his shoulder, his stomach dropping when he saw a group of men a few paces back. There were six of them, their silhouettes hulking and dark under the dim streetlights, moving with a deliberate slowness that sent a chill through Simon's spine.

Matthew followed Simon's gaze, and his smile faltered.

The footsteps behind them quickened, and Simon's pulse spiked. His grip tightened around Matthew's arm.

"Let's just keep walking," Matthew whispered, his voice steady but laced with tension. "We'll be fine."

But as the men closed in, it became clear that walking wasn't going to be enough.

"Oi!" one of the men called out, his voice sharp and mocking. "Where you two off to, eh?"

Simon froze, his breath catching in his throat. He could feel Matthew tense beside him, his body bristling with the same fear Simon felt deep in his bones. They didn't need to turn around to know what was coming next.

"Look at them, holding hands and all," another one of the men sneered. "Proper couple of queers."

The words hit Simon like a punch to the gut, and before he could respond, the men were right behind them. The first shove came out of nowhere—Matthew stumbled forward, catching himself before turning around to face them, his eyes blazing with anger.

"Leave us alone," Matthew said, his voice firm.

But the men only laughed, circling them like predators sizing up their prey.

"Leave us alone?" one of them mocked. He was tall, with broad shoulders and a leering grin that made Simon's skin crawl. "Why should we? Just want to have a chat with you two lovebirds."

Matthew stepped in front of Simon, his body a shield between them and the gang. Simon's heart pounded in his chest, his mind racing. He knew what was coming next.

"Don't," Matthew warned, his voice low, almost pleading. "Just let us go."

It was at this point, now that the men stood before them in this dimly lit street, that Simon noticed that these were not men; this was a gang of scruffy boys around the same age as them.

The leader of the group sneered, his eyes narrowing. "Or what? You'll kiss us to death?"

The boys erupted into cruel laughter, and Simon felt the fear turn into something sharper, more primal. He reached for Matthew's hand, gripping it tightly, trying to steady himself.

But then the first punch was thrown.

It happened so fast, Simon barely registered it. One moment, they were standing there, hearts pounding, and the next, Matthew was shoved backward, his head snapping to the side as the blow landed across his face. He stumbled, and before Simon could react, one of the boys grabbed him by the arm, yanking him away from Matthew.

Panic surged through Simon as he struggled against the boy's grip, his eyes darting toward Matthew, who was already being swarmed by two of the others.

"No!" Simon shouted, but his voice was drowned out by the chaos around them.

Another punch. Matthew fell to the ground, and the boys descended on him, their fists and feet flying in a brutal assault. Simon felt like he was watching from a distance, his vision blurring as he saw Matthew's body curl into itself, trying to protect himself from the relentless blows.

Simon wrenched himself free from the boy holding him and lunged toward Matthew, but another one of the attackers stepped in his way, shoving him back hard. Simon hit the pavement, the rough concrete scraping his palms, but he scrambled to his feet, desperate to reach Matthew.

"Run!" Matthew shouted, his voice choked with pain.

Simon hesitated, his body frozen in place for a split second. He couldn't just leave him—he couldn't leave Matthew behind. But they were relentless, their fists and feet pounding into Matthew with sickening force.

"Run!" Matthew shouted again, his voice breaking.

Simon's instincts took over, and he turned and ran.

His feet pounded against the pavement as he sprinted down the street, his breath ragged in his throat. He could hear the boy behind him, their voices raised in angry shouts as they gave chase. His mind was a blur of terror and guilt—he was running, but Matthew was still back there, still trapped beneath their fists.

And then he heard it. A sharp, gut-wrenching scream.

Simon glanced over his shoulder, his heart stopping as he saw one of the boys lunge toward Matthew, a glint of silver in his hand.

The knife.

The blade flashed in the dim light, and before Simon could comprehend what was happening, it plunged into Matthew's side. Time seemed to slow as Matthew's body jolted, his eyes wide with shock and pain. The world tilted, everything spinning out of control as Matthew crumpled to the ground.

"No!" Simon screamed, his voice tearing through the night.

The gang scattered, their laughter and taunts echoing in Simon's ears as they fled into the shadows, leaving Matthew lying motionless on the pavement. Simon's legs buckled beneath him, but he forced himself forward, stumbling toward Matthew's still form.

Chapter 9
THE FALL

The sound of Simon's feet pounding against the pavement was drowned out by the ragged breath tearing through his throat. He couldn't think—couldn't process what had just happened. All he knew was that Matthew was lying on the ground, blood pooling beneath him, his face contorted in pain.

Simon fell to his knees beside him, his hands trembling as they hovered over Matthew's body, unsure where to touch, unsure how to help.

"Matthew," Simon gasped, his voice broken. "Matthew, please."

Matthew's eyes fluttered open, and for a brief moment, Simon saw the boy he loved, the boy who had made him feel like the world was worth living in. But that light was fading fast, replaced by a hollow, vacant look that sent a wave of terror crashing over Simon.

Blood soaked Matthew's shirt, seeping through the fabric in dark, wet patches that spread across his side. Simon pressed his hands to the wound, trying desperately to stop the bleeding, but it kept coming, thick and unrelenting, slipping through his fingers.

"It's okay," Matthew whispered, his voice so faint Simon could barely hear it. "I'm... okay."

But he wasn't. Simon could see the life draining out of him, could feel the warmth leaving his body as the blood continued to pour from the wound. The knife had done its damage—Simon knew it, even if he didn't want to admit it.

"Don't... don't say that," Simon choked out, his hands trembling as he pressed harder, trying to stem the flow of blood. "You're going to be fine. I'm going to get help."

But there was no one around. The streets were deserted, the sounds of the city far away from the hell Simon was living in. He fumbled for his phone, his hands slick with Matthew's blood, trying to dial emergency services.

Matthew's breath was growing shallower, each exhale a struggle. His eyes fluttered shut, and Simon's heart seized in his chest.

"Stay with me," Simon begged, his voice breaking. "Please, Matthew, stay with me."

But Matthew's body was going limp beneath him, his breathing slowing to a faint whisper. Simon's phone slipped from his bloodied hands as he pressed his forehead to Matthew's, his tears mingling with the blood on Matthew's skin.

"I love you," Simon whispered, his voice raw with grief. "Please... don't leave me."

The distant wail of sirens pierced the night, but it was too late.

Matthew's body went still in Simon's arms, his breath fading into nothingness.

Simon's world shattered around him, the weight of his grief so heavy it felt like he was drowning. The world around Simon blurred, the sound of the sirens growing louder, but none of it mattered. He was alone in this moment, alone with the boy he loved lying lifeless in his arms. Matthew's blood soaked through Simon's clothes, warm and sticky, but Simon couldn't let go. He couldn't move.

He couldn't breathe.

"Matthew?" Simon's voice cracked, barely more than a whisper, as he shook him gently, as if that would somehow pull him back. As if his love alone could will Matthew's heart to beat again. "Please... come back."

But there was no answer. The quiet street, the stillness of the night—it all pressed down on him, suffocating. The harsh blue and red lights of an approaching ambulance flashed against the brick walls, but they were too late. They were always going to be too late.

Voices began to fill the silence, paramedics rushing toward him, their voices urgent, though Simon couldn't make out the words. His entire world was the lifeless body in his arms, the boy who had once been his everything, now reduced to silence and stillness.

"Sir, we need you to let go," one of the paramedics said, crouching beside Simon, their hands gentle as they tried to pull him away from Matthew.

But Simon couldn't. He couldn't let go. He clung to Matthew's shirt, his fingers twisted in the blood-soaked fabric, his body shaking with sobs that felt too big for him to contain. His chest heaved with the weight of the grief that had already begun to suffocate him, wrapping around his heart like a vice.

"I can't," Simon choked out, his voice raw. "I can't leave him."

The paramedic exchanged a glance with their partner before leaning closer, their hand resting on Simon's shoulder. "I know this is hard, but we need to help him now. We need to do our job."

Simon looked down at Matthew, his face pale, lips slightly parted as if he were only sleeping. But the unnatural stillness of his body, the dark red spreading beneath him, told Simon the truth. Matthew wasn't sleeping. He wasn't going to wake up.

Somehow, Simon's hands released their grip, and he felt himself being pulled gently back by the paramedics. He sat on the pavement, his arms limp at his sides, watching in a numb haze as the team worked over Matthew's body. Their movements were quick, methodical, but Simon knew—he knew it was futile.

One of the paramedics pressed their hands to Matthew's chest, starting compressions, their face set in grim determination. Another began shouting into a radio, calling for additional support, but their voices felt distant, like they were underwater, muffled and far away.

Simon watched in silence, his body feeling disconnected from his mind. He was aware of everything–the flashing lights, the cold night air biting at his skin, the wetness of Matthew's blood soaking through his clothes–but none of it felt real. It was as though he was floating outside himself, watching this nightmare unfold from somewhere far away.

He wanted to scream. He wanted to run. He wanted to wake up from this horrible dream and find himself back in Matthew's arms, safe and whole. But all Simon could do was sit there, trembling, his tears blurring the scene in front of him.

Minutes stretched into eternity as the paramedics worked. The night closed in, the weight of it suffocating. Simon's vision swam, and his chest ached with every ragged breath.

"Come on, Matthew," one of the paramedics muttered under their breath as they continued compressions. "Come on."

But there was no movement. No spark of life. The world remained still, unmoving, as Matthew lay there, silent and unresponsive.

After what felt like a lifetime, the paramedics stopped. The hands that had been pressing into Matthew's chest slowed, then fell away. Simon watched, his breath catching in his throat, as they exchanged glances, their faces etched with sorrow.

One of the paramedics knelt in front of Simon, their voice soft, though the words sliced through Simon's already shattered heart. "I'm so sorry… we did everything we could."

Simon's entire body seemed to collapse inward, the weight of the words breaking him in a way he hadn't thought possible. The world around him faded to nothing, and the only sound he could hear was the echo of his own heart, breaking over and over again.

Matthew was gone.

Simon couldn't feel the ground beneath him anymore. He couldn't feel anything. The sobs that tore through him were raw, unrelenting, as the reality of it hit him with full force.

Matthew was gone.

Gone, and he wasn't coming back.

Simon wrapped his arms around himself, trying to hold on to something–anything–but there was nothing left to hold. His world, his future, had been ripped away from him in a single, violent moment, leaving him empty and broken.

And in that moment, Simon knew that nothing would ever be the same again.

Chapter 10
LOST

In the days that followed Matthew's death, Simon felt as though he was floating in a haze, drifting through a world that no longer made sense. It was as though time had slowed, each hour dragging painfully, each moment heavy with the absence of the one person who had meant everything to him. The vibrant, joyful existence he had once shared with Matthew felt like a distant memory, something too fragile to have ever been real.

Simon had always known grief was painful, but this? This was something else. It was as though a part of him had died that night too, ripped away and left to bleed out on the cold, unforgiving pavement. Every breath was a reminder that Matthew would never take another. Every second that ticked by without him felt like a betrayal.

His parents did their best to comfort him, but their words were empty, like trying to fix a shattered vase with a single bandage. His mum would sit beside him, her hand resting on his shoulder, her voice soft and pleading. "Simon, please talk to us. We're worried about you."

But Simon couldn't talk. He didn't know how to explain what it felt like to lose someone who had been his entire world. The emptiness inside him was too vast, too consuming to put into words. Every time he tried to speak, to explain the unbearable weight pressing on his chest, he felt like he was suffocating.

The guilt was worse than the sadness. It gnawed at him, relentless and unforgiving. He couldn't shake the memory of that night–Matthew's desperate shouts for him to run, the sound of that knife cutting through the air, the sickening thud of Matthew's body hitting the ground. And Simon had run. He had left him behind.

What if I had stayed? What if I had fought harder?

Those questions haunted him, playing on a loop in his mind. They echoed in the silence of his room, in the early morning hours when the house was still and dark, when his thoughts were the loudest and most cruel. Simon would lie awake at night, staring at the ceiling, Matthew's face burned into his mind. The memory of Matthew smiling, laughing, living, now replaced by the image of him lying still, lifeless, as the paramedics worked in vain to save him.

Simon's days blurred together. He barely left his room, unable to face the world without Matthew. The vibrant colours of life had faded into dull, grey monotones, and Simon couldn't find the energy to care about anything. His parents were worried–he could hear them talking in hushed tones when they thought he wasn't listening–but their concern felt like another layer of guilt, another weight to carry.

Sometimes he'd walk to the places he and Matthew had shared–the beach, the park, even the pub where they'd spent so many nights together, laughing and talking about a future that would never come. Each place felt hollow now, as though it had been stripped of its meaning, a ghostly reminder of what he had lost. The world seemed cruel in its indifference, moving forward while Simon was stuck in an endless loop of that one night, reliving the moment Matthew's life had been stolen.

School was unbearable. Everyone knew. The whispers followed him down every corridor, the sympathetic glances from teachers, the pity in the eyes of his classmates. But it wasn't just pity. There was something else, too–an uncomfortable avoidance, a reluctance to acknowledge what had happened to him. It was as though the mere mention of Matthew's name was too much, too raw for anyone to touch. Simon's friends tried to be supportive at first, but they quickly realised that no words could reach him.

He was drowning, and there was no lifeline.

One afternoon, a week after the funeral, Simon found himself standing in front of the mirror in his bedroom. His reflection stared back at him, hollow-eyed and gaunt. He didn't recognise himself. He looked like a stranger, someone who had been emptied out, the shell of a boy who had once known love and joy. His eyes were bloodshot, his face pale. He had stopped caring about how he looked, how he smelled, how he presented himself to the world. What was the point? The one person who had ever seen him, truly seen him, was gone.

And he hadn't been able to save him.

Simon clenched his fists, his nails digging into his palms until they drew blood. But the pain didn't register. Nothing registered. He was numb, lost in the depths of his grief, consumed by the knowledge that Matthew had died because of him—because he had run. He had left him behind. The guilt gnawed at him, eating him alive from the inside out.

He punched the wall, the impact jarring but offering no relief. Another punch, and then another, until his knuckles were raw and bruised. But still, the pain inside him remained, festering like a wound that would never heal.

Chapter 11
FURY IN THE SILENCE

After weeks of suffocating under the weight of his grief, a new emotion began to bubble beneath the surface–rage. At first, it was a quiet, simmering anger, a feeling that gnawed at the edges of his sorrow. But as the days passed, the anger grew louder, more insistent, until it threatened to consume him entirely.

Matthew's killer had never been caught.

The gang that had attacked them that night had vanished into the shadows, slipping through the cracks of the city like phantoms. The police had taken Simon's statement, promised they would investigate, but days turned into weeks, and there was no news, no progress. Every time Simon called for an update, he was met with vague assurances, hollow words that did nothing to ease the burning fury inside him.

The injustice of it all made Simon feel like he was coming apart at the seams. Matthew was dead. His life had been stolen from him in a single, brutal moment, and the people responsible were still out there, living their lives as though nothing had happened. As though Matthew's life meant nothing.

The anger became all-consuming. It filled every corner of Simon's mind, pushing out the grief, the guilt, until all that remained was a burning desire for justice. He couldn't sit by and do nothing. He couldn't let Matthew's death be another statistic, another unsolved case that would eventually fade from people's memories.

One afternoon, after yet another fruitless call with the police, Simon stormed out of the house, his chest heaving with frustration. His parents had tried to stop him, their concerned voices trailing behind him as he slammed the door, but Simon couldn't listen to them anymore. He couldn't listen to anyone. All he wanted was to find those men—to confront them, to make them pay for what they had done.

He found himself walking through the streets of Bournemouth, his eyes scanning every face, every alleyway, looking for the slightest hint of familiarity. He didn't even know what he was looking for—he hadn't seen the gang clearly enough to recognise them, but the need for vengeance pulsed through him like a heartbeat. He wandered aimlessly, his fists clenched at his sides, his mind racing with thoughts of what he would do if he found them.

But deep down, he knew it was hopeless. The town was too big, too anonymous. The boys who had taken Matthew from him could be anyone, anywhere. And that knowledge—that crushing realisation—only made Simon's rage burn hotter.

He began spending his nights trawling the streets, searching for something he couldn't name. The anger drove him forward, kept him moving even when his body screamed for rest. He wanted to fight. He wanted to hurt someone the way he had been hurt. He wanted to make the world feel the same pain that had been tearing him apart since the night Matthew died.

One evening, Simon found himself outside the pub where they had been before the attack. The memories flooded back, sharp and vivid–the warmth of Matthew's hand in his, the sound of his laughter, the way they had walked down this very street, completely unaware of the danger lurking just ahead.

Simon clenched his jaw, his eyes burning with unshed tears. He wanted to smash something, to break the world apart the way his had been broken. But instead, he stood there, shaking with rage, his hands trembling at his sides.

As the anger coursed through him, something shifted. Simon realised that the rage wasn't just directed at the boys who had killed Matthew–it was directed at the world, at the system that had failed them both. The police weren't doing enough. The city didn't care. Matthew had been murdered, and yet life continued as if nothing had happened.

No one cared. No one except Simon.

He couldn't let this go. He couldn't let Matthew's death be forgotten, swept under the rug by a society that would rather pretend it never happened. The thought of those boys living their lives, laughing with their friends, sleeping in their beds, while Matthew was buried in the cold ground–it was unbearable.

The fire inside Simon burned brighter than ever, the flames licking at the edges of his sanity. He needed justice. He needed to do something. Anything.

But as Simon stood there, trembling with rage, he realised something else: no matter how hard he fought, no matter how much anger he carried with him, it wouldn't bring Matthew back. The hole in his heart would never be filled. The love of his life was gone, and there was nothing he could do to change that.

The injustice of it all was a weight he would carry with him for the rest of his life.

But that didn't mean he would stop fighting.

Chapter 12
NEW BEGINNINGS

After the devastating loss of Matthew, Portsmouth offered Simon a chance at something he desperately needed–a fresh start. Moving to the city to attend university was a decision made with careful thought, both by him and his parents. They all agreed that distance, a new environment, and new experiences might help Simon begin to heal, or at least find some distance from the tragedy that had shaped the end of his teenage years.

Portsmouth, with its mix of vibrant student life and coastal charm, was a world away from the heavy memories of Bournemouth. The city bustled with life, with its lively waterfront, cafés full of students, and the constant hum of energy that came with university life. Simon's new world at university was full of possibilities. And while he knew that leaving the past behind wasn't truly possible, he hoped that, in this new place, he could at least start to rebuild himself.

Settling into halls was a strange experience for Simon. The small room felt stark at first, a blank slate with none of the familiarity of home. The walls were bare, and the bed felt too stiff. But it also represented freedom—a place where no one knew him as the boy who had lost someone. No one whispered about the tragic events of his past. He was just another student in the bustling crowd, free to define himself in new ways.

For the first few weeks, Simon kept his head down. He threw himself into his studies, immersing himself in the academic side of university life. The rhythm of lectures, assignments, and late-night study sessions was comforting in its predictability. It was something to focus on, something to keep his mind occupied. His course was challenging, but that was part of the appeal. The more he buried himself in his work, the less time he had to dwell on the past.

But the social side of university was harder to navigate. Simon had never been particularly outgoing, and after what had happened with Matthew, the idea of opening up to new people—of trusting them—felt impossible. The university had a well-established LGBT group that ran events and organised trips to pride celebrations, and while Simon occasionally went along, he mostly stayed on the fringes. It was comforting to know the group was there, to see people like him living freely and openly, but he still couldn't bring himself to fully engage. He wasn't ready for that.

He made a few friends—people from his course or his halls who were nice enough. They'd sit together in the dining hall or head out to the pub after class, but Simon always kept his distance. Whenever one of those friendships seemed to hint at something more, something deeper, Simon would retreat behind his carefully constructed walls. He'd mastered the art of keeping people at arm's length, of engaging just enough to seem present but never vulnerable.

When one of his friends, Jake, a fellow student from the LGBT group, suggested grabbing a drink together after a particularly successful event, Simon felt a flicker of something—maybe interest, maybe possibility—but as the night wore on, that flicker was quickly extinguished. Jake was nice, attractive even, and there was chemistry there, but Simon wasn't ready. Not yet.

He always felt the need to push back against anything that felt too close, too intimate. The ghost of Matthew still haunted him, and Simon couldn't shake the feeling that letting someone in again would only lead to more pain.

Months passed in this half-life, where Simon was present but never fully engaged. He went on the occasional date, meeting guys for coffee or drinks, but it never felt like more than going through the motions. He'd talk, laugh, maybe flirt a little, but when things threatened to get physical or emotional, Simon would pull away. Even when the dates led to more—an invitation back to their place, a brief kiss at the end of the night—Simon always found a way to stop it before it went too far. The idea of intimacy still frightened him, not just physically but emotionally. He wasn't ready to give himself to someone again, not like that.

It was lonely at times, and frustrating. Simon knew he was holding back, that he was stopping himself from living the life he wanted. He had built a wall around himself so thick, so impenetrable, that sometimes it felt like he was suffocating behind it.

But something had to change.

One evening, after yet another night of sitting in his room, scrolling mindlessly through his phone, Simon realised that he couldn't keep living like this. He couldn't keep holding back, waiting for something to happen without ever taking the risk to make it happen. He had to start living his life again, truly living it, not just existing within the safety of his own isolation.

So, he pushed himself.

He forced himself to attend more LGBT events, to be more social, to engage with people in a way that felt uncomfortable but necessary. He joined study groups, went to more parties, and even let himself flirt a little more openly. It wasn't easy–every step forward felt like dragging himself through mud–but it was progress.

He made more friends, real friends this time. People like Katie, a fiercely passionate film student who shared his love of literature and who always seemed to know exactly what to say to make him laugh. There was also Tom, a history major with a quiet wit and a talent for finding the best hidden spots in the city. These new connections felt different–easier somehow–because Simon was allowing himself to let people in, just a little bit more.

But still, Simon was waiting. He was waiting for that spark, for the right person to come along, the one who would make him feel ready to try again. Ready to open his heart in a way that didn't feel forced or too soon. Someone who would make him believe that love, real love, was possible again.

And then, one night at a university social event, Simon met Andrew.

Andrew was everything Simon had been waiting for without even realising it. There was an ease between them from the very beginning–an instant connection that felt both exciting and natural. They started off with casual meetups, grabbing coffee between lectures, laughing about how much coursework they had or debating which of the local pubs had the best atmosphere. There was chemistry between them, undeniable but unspoken at first.

Simon felt himself slowly lowering his guard around Andrew, though the barriers were still there, cautious and carefully maintained. But Andrew was patient. He never pushed too hard, never demanded more than Simon was willing to give. And that patience, that quiet understanding, was what made Simon feel like, maybe, this time would be different.

As their friendship deepened, Simon found himself thinking about Andrew more and more. There was something about him that felt... promising. Maybe it was the way he seemed genuinely interested in Simon's life, his past, his passions. Maybe it was the way Andrew could make him laugh, even on days when Simon felt like retreating into himself. Or maybe it was just that, for the first time since Matthew, Simon felt like he was ready to try again.

To let someone in.

It wasn't perfect. Simon still held back, still had moments of hesitation, of doubt. He wasn't sure he would ever be completely free of the fear that had settled inside him after Matthew's death. But with Andrew, things felt different. Slowly, cautiously, Simon allowed himself to hope again.

He had spent so long waiting for the right person, for the right moment, and now, for the first time, Simon felt like maybe—just maybe—he had found it.

And Andrew looked promising.

Chapter 13
HEALING IN THE FIRE

As the present unfolded, Simon found himself navigating new territory with Andrew. There was a cautious optimism in their growing relationship, a sense that this might be something different, something worth holding on to. Yet, no matter how hard Simon tried to stay grounded in the moment, the weight of his past still lingered. The ghost of Matthew was never far from his mind, especially now, as he began opening himself up again—both emotionally and intimately.

Andrew had a way of making Simon feel at ease, something that had become increasingly rare in his life. Their relationship evolved naturally, from tentative coffee dates to long nights spent talking, laughing, and discovering more about each other. But with every step forward, Simon was acutely aware of how different this felt from anything he'd experienced since Matthew. Andrew wasn't just someone he was trying to get to know—he was someone who had the potential to help Simon heal.

One evening, after a night out with friends, the chemistry between them became impossible to ignore. They were back at Andrew's flat, the tension that had been simmering for weeks finally bubbling over. Simon felt the heat of Andrew's gaze as they stood close, and before he knew it, they were kissing—hungry, desperate kisses that spoke of pent-up desire and something deeper. For the first time in a long time, Simon allowed himself to fully feel it, to let go of the walls he had been holding up for so long.

As they moved together, Simon felt both exhilarated and vulnerable. It wasn't just the physical intimacy that made him nervous—it was the emotional openness that came with it. They spent hours exploring each other, learning what they liked, what they didn't, the intensity of their connection growing with every touch, every kiss. Andrew was patient, intuitive, always aware of Simon's needs and boundaries. It was different from anything Simon had known before, and that difference both excited and scared him.

They found a rhythm together, discovering each other's sexual preferences in a way that was playful but intimate. Andrew liked to take his time, while Simon discovered he enjoyed being pushed just enough to feel that edge of excitement. Their nights together were hot and intense, their bodies in sync as they explored new layers of passion. It was as though they were creating their own language— one of desire, trust, and vulnerability.

Yet, in the heat of the moment, Simon's mind would sometimes drift. Flashes of memory would surface—memories of Matthew, of their nights together, of the connection they had shared. It wasn't that Simon was comparing Andrew to Matthew, but rather that the past was a part of him, woven into every decision, every feeling. When Andrew suggested they hit the clubs and dance late into the night, Simon agreed, though he hadn't expected how much it would stir up those old memories.

One night, they found themselves in a dark, sweaty club, the music pounding in their ears, the air thick with energy. The flashing lights, the thumping bass–it all reminded Simon of the nights he and Matthew had spent together at DYMK, where they had once danced until their legs ached, bodies pressed together as if the rest of the world didn't exist.

Andrew, full of life and excitement, tugged off his shirt and grinned at Simon. "Come on," he urged, his voice barely audible over the music. "Let's just enjoy this."

Simon hesitated for only a moment before he followed Andrew's lead, stripping off his own shirt and joining him on the dance floor. The feel of Andrew's skin against his, the heat of their bodies as they danced together–it brought back those memories of Matthew, but not in a way that hurt. Instead, it felt like reclaiming something, like he was finally allowing himself to create new memories without erasing the old ones.

They danced for hours, lost in the music, lost in each other. Sweat slicked their skin, their movements in perfect sync as they let go of everything except the moment. For the first time in a long time, Simon felt alive, truly alive, as if the weight he had been carrying for so long had started to lift.

Afterwards, as they stumbled out of the club, breathless and laughing, Andrew threw an arm around Simon's shoulders. "That was insane," he said, his eyes sparkling with the excitement of the night. "We've gotta do that again."

Simon smiled, his heart swelling with a strange mix of joy and bittersweetness. It had been Andrew's idea to dance like that, to lose themselves in the heat of the night, but it had felt so familiar, like a bridge between his past and his present. And in that moment, Simon realised that maybe that was okay. Maybe it was okay to let the past and the present coexist, to honour what he had lost while still allowing himself to move forward.

As their relationship deepened, Simon found himself growing more comfortable with Andrew, more willing to open up in ways he hadn't thought possible. They spent weekends together, sometimes just curled up on the sofa, talking about everything from their childhoods to their future plans. Andrew was good at listening, at giving Simon the space to share his thoughts and feelings without judgement. And slowly, Simon began to let those walls come down.

One night, as they lay in bed together, Andrew traced a finger along Simon's arm, his voice soft in the quiet of the room. "I know you've been through a lot, Simon. You don't have to talk about it if you're not ready, but... I'm here. Whenever you are."

Simon's chest tightened with emotion, the weight of Matthew's memory pressing against him. But instead of retreating into himself, as he had so many times before, he turned to Andrew, meeting his gaze.

"I loved him," Simon whispered, his voice barely audible. "Matthew. I loved him, and... I lost him."

Andrew didn't say anything, didn't press for more. He simply nodded, his hand slipping into Simon's, his grip steady and reassuring.

"I'm not… trying to replace him," Simon continued, his throat tight with the effort of speaking the words he had kept buried for so long. "But being with you… it's helping. I didn't think I'd ever be able to feel this again."

Andrew leaned in, pressing a soft kiss to Simon's forehead. "You don't have to rush anything," he murmured. "We'll go at your pace."

And in that moment, Simon knew that Andrew was different. He wasn't just a distraction or a fleeting connection—he was someone who saw Simon, who understood the scars he carried and was willing to help him heal. With Andrew, there was no pressure, no expectation. Just the steady, growing feeling that maybe, just maybe, Simon could find love again.

Their romance was a mix of passion and tenderness, of new experiences and old memories. Simon was still cautious, still carrying the weight of his past, but with Andrew, he was learning to let go. He was learning that it was possible to create new memories, to love someone without losing the part of him that would always love Matthew.

And as the nights blurred into mornings, and their relationship blossomed, Simon felt the stirrings of something he hadn't felt in a long time.

Hope.

Chapter 14
UNSETTLING CLUES

Things had been going well–really well, in fact. Simon found himself smiling more, laughing at Andrew's ridiculous jokes, feeling a warmth and lightness that he hadn't experienced in years. Their relationship was blossoming, each day bringing a new sense of connection and trust. But, as with everything in Simon's life, shadows from the past were never too far behind.

It started innocently enough, a throwaway comment from Andrew one afternoon while they were walking along the Portsmouth seafront.

"Did I ever tell you I'm from Bournemouth too?" Andrew said casually, as though it were just a passing detail.

Simon paused for a moment, surprised. "No, I don't think you mentioned that before."

"Yeah, West Howe," Andrew added, kicking a stone along the path. "Bit rough round the edges, to be honest. Definitely not the best part of town."

Simon's heart gave a small jolt at the mention of Bournemouth, but he brushed it off quickly. Bournemouth wasn't a small town; hundreds of thousands of people lived there. It was entirely possible, maybe even likely, that they had never crossed paths before. After all, Simon's Bournemouth felt worlds away from whatever life Andrew had lived there.

"Oh, right," Simon said, trying to keep his tone light. "I'm from a different part of town. Southbourne."

Andrew nodded, as though the details weren't of much interest. "Yeah, it's funny we never bumped into each other, though. I used to go into the town centre a lot. Me and my mates would hang around The Square, Westover Road, you know, the usual places. Did you ever go out much back then?"

Simon shrugged, forcing a smile. "Not really. I wasn't into the scene much." The mention of The Square tugged at something deep in his memory, but he quickly pushed it aside. Bournemouth was full of people. The chances that Andrew knew anything about his past–about that night–were slim to none.

But even as they continued walking, Andrew's words stuck with him, small hooks snagging in the back of Simon's mind. He tried to shake it off, tried to remind himself that Andrew didn't know. Couldn't know.

That night, as they lay in bed together, Andrew wrapped his arm around Simon's waist, pulling him close. Simon felt the familiar comfort of Andrew's warmth, his steady presence. But for the first time in a long while, Simon felt a flicker of unease.

Over the following weeks, Andrew's comments about Bournemouth seemed to crop up more and more often. It wasn't intentional, Simon thought—Andrew wasn't being careless or trying to pry—but every time he mentioned something about his past, it stirred an uncomfortable sensation deep within Simon's chest.

One evening, they were sitting in a café, laughing about something trivial when Andrew brought up his mates from back home. "Yeah, those were some wild days. We'd just hang around the town centre, go down to the beach sometimes... But it wasn't always fun, y'know? Some of the lads I hung around with weren't the best people."

Simon frowned, stirring his coffee. "What do you mean?"

Andrew hesitated for a moment, his eyes shifting toward the window as if he were carefully choosing his words. "I mean... back then, I wasn't out, obviously. None of my mates knew, and, well... they weren't exactly fans of anyone who was. Some of them were... rough. They'd pick on people."

"People like who?" Simon asked, his voice low, a strange tension creeping into his chest.

Andrew shrugged, looking uncomfortable. "Gays. Anyone who seemed different, really. It was stupid, and I hated it, but I had to go along with it. I couldn't be the one who stood out, you know? It's not like I had a choice. If I didn't join in, I'd be their next target."

Simon's heart skipped a beat. His hand froze around his mug, the warmth of the coffee suddenly distant as his thoughts churned. There was something too familiar in Andrew's words, something that made the hairs on the back of his neck stand up.

"Did you… did you ever actually hurt anyone?" Simon asked carefully, his stomach twisting.

Andrew shook his head quickly, looking almost ashamed. "No. God, no. I just… stood by. It was easier to keep my mouth shut, act like I was just one of them. If they didn't see me as different, I was safe. It was survival back then, y'know? But I hated it. I hated every second of it."

Simon wanted to believe him. He did believe him. But something about the way Andrew talked about those days, about the town centre, about blending in with a group that picked on gay people—it gnawed at him.

-

The first real crack came one weekend when they were lounging around at Andrew's flat, binge-watching a TV series. Andrew, half-asleep, started talking about Bournemouth again. Simon's ears perked up at the mention of Westover Road.

"We used to hang around there all the time, late at night," Andrew said lazily, stretching out on the couch. "The lads loved causing trouble. God, it was ridiculous. They'd get into fights, steal stuff. They'd even go down to the beach sometimes and just… terrorise people."

Simon's stomach dropped.

He sat up a little straighter, his heart racing as Andrew's words sank in. Westover Road. That was where it had happened. The Square, the beach. The same places Matthew and Simon had walked through that night. Simon felt the air around him grow thick and heavy, his breathing shallow as memories began to resurface.

He had tried so hard not to think about that night. But now, with Andrew casually mentioning places that were so intimately tied to his worst memories, it felt like those moments were rising to the surface, demanding to be acknowledged.

"You guys… just went around picking fights?" Simon asked, trying to keep his voice steady, even though his insides were twisting.

Andrew shrugged. "Not me. I just watched. It was stupid. But the lads were always looking for someone to hassle. They'd go after anyone–drunks, homeless people, gay couples… It was horrible. But like I said, I wasn't out back then. I couldn't exactly stop them."

Simon stared at him, the weight of Andrew's words pressing down on him like a vice. He wanted to ask more, to dig deeper, but he wasn't sure he was ready for what he might find. What would he do if Andrew had been there that night? If Andrew had known–or worse, been part of–the group that had attacked him and Matthew?

"Do you ever think about it?" Simon asked softly, trying to keep his voice calm. "About what they did to those people?"

Andrew sighed, rubbing a hand over his face. "Yeah. I do. I hate that I didn't stop it. I hate that I was even part of that group. But back then, it was survival. I didn't have the strength to stand up to them."

Simon nodded, but his mind was racing. The timeline wasn't clear yet, and Andrew didn't seem to know about the attack. He didn't know about Matthew–at least, not the full story. But with every conversation, more and more pieces were falling into place, and Simon couldn't shake the growing suspicion that Andrew had been closer to that night than he realised.

One evening, Simon and Andrew were sitting in a bar after a long day. The atmosphere was relaxed, the soft hum of conversation around them a soothing background to their quiet talk. Andrew was telling Simon about the beach in Bournemouth, how he and his mates used to hang out there late at night, getting drunk, causing trouble.

"They used to love running around in the dark, chasing people off," Andrew said with a grimace. "I hated it. But, y'know, I had to keep my head down, had to pretend to be like them."

Simon's breath caught in his throat.

"What do you mean, chasing people off?" he asked, his voice tighter than he intended.

Andrew sighed, his expression serious. "They were just bullies, really. They'd see a couple–anyone who looked like they didn't belong–and harass them. Especially if they were gay. They'd yell insults, throw things, sometimes even get violent."

The words hit Simon like a punch to the gut, his mind was racing, heart pounding in his chest as flashes of that night flooded back–running, the shouts behind them, Matthew's voice telling him to run, the brutal sound of fists and feet connecting with Matthew's body, and the glint of the knife.

He couldn't breathe. Couldn't think.

Andrew, unaware of Simon's inner turmoil, took another sip of his drink and leaned back in his chair. "Bournemouth was a rough place for me. I didn't know who I was back then. Didn't know how to stand up for myself. I just went along with whatever the lads did."

Simon's hand tightened around his glass, his knuckles turning white.

The pieces were falling into place, each comment, each memory, lining up in a way that Simon couldn't ignore. Andrew had been there–maybe not involved directly, but he had been close. Too close. The group that had attacked

Matthew... the beach, the town centre, the way they'd chased people off... It all matched too perfectly with what Andrew was describing.

Simon's stomach churned, and he felt a wave of nausea wash over him. He didn't want to believe it. He couldn't. Andrew wasn't like that now. He wasn't violent, he wasn't cruel. But if Andrew had been part of that group, if he had stood by while his mates had attacked people like him and Matthew...

What if Andrew had been there that night?

The thought made Simon's blood run cold.

He had to know more. He had to be sure.

Chapter 15

SUSPICIONS GROW

The warmth and comfort Simon had found with Andrew was now tainted by a creeping paranoia he couldn't shake. Every smile, every touch, every shared laugh now felt fragile, underpinned by the gnawing question that refused to leave Simon's mind: Was Andrew involved in Matthew's attack?

The idea had first seemed absurd. Impossible. But the more Simon replayed Andrew's offhand comments about his past, the more those puzzle pieces fell into place. The references to Bournemouth, the nights spent with rough friends in The Square, Westover Road, and the beach–the same areas where Simon and Matthew had walked that night–all began to align in a way that left Simon feeling sick to his stomach.

Simon had told Andrew about Matthew before, but only in broad strokes. Cautiously only sharing the basics: how he and Matthew had been attacked one night, and how Matthew had been killed in the aftermath. He hadn't gone into specifics–hadn't told Andrew exactly where it happened, when, or the brutal details of how Matthew had been stabbed and left to die on the cold pavement. The story had been vague, a necessary glossing over of the trauma, enough to explain his guardedness without revealing the depth of his pain. Andrew had listened with quiet understanding, expressing sympathy but never prying for more. And while Simon had appreciated that, there was always a small part of him that wondered, Did Andrew know more than he let on? With each passing conversation, with every casual mention of Andrew's past in Bournemouth, Simon's mind raced. There was still a chance that Andrew had nothing to do with Matthew's death, that the overlap in their stories was just a painful coincidence. But what if he did?

He needed to know the truth.

But confronting Andrew directly wasn't an option. Andrew didn't seem to remember the specific details of the attacks, didn't connect his past with the attack that had ripped Simon's life apart. And Simon wasn't ready to reveal the depths of his suspicions—not yet, not until he had something concrete. So, Simon did the only thing he could think of: he started recording their conversations.

It started small. Simon installed a discreet voice recorder app on his phone, tucking it in his pocket during casual conversations with Andrew. The first time he hit record, he felt a pang of guilt, as if he were betraying the trust that had blossomed between them. But the need for answers, for justice, was stronger than the guilt.

Each time they sat together—whether it was over a quiet dinner, lounging on the sofa, or walking through the city—Simon would steer the conversation ever so subtly back toward Bournemouth, hoping Andrew might slip up, might offer some detail that would confirm his darkest fears.

The psychological toll of this double life began to weigh on Simon. He found himself caught between two conflicting emotions: the growing affection he had for Andrew and the simmering rage that bubbled up every time Andrew mentioned his past. He cared for Andrew–there was no denying that–but how could he reconcile his feelings for someone who might have been complicit in Matthew's death?

One evening, as they sat together watching TV, Simon casually brought up Bournemouth again, trying to keep his tone light.

"So, you never go back to visit home, do you?" Simon asked, shifting slightly on the couch, his fingers brushing against the phone in his pocket, where the recorder was already running.

Andrew shrugged, his eyes on the screen. "Not really. There's nothing for me there anymore. My family's moved out of West Howe, and I don't keep in touch with the old crowd. Besides, Portsmouth's more like home now."

Simon nodded, keeping his expression neutral. "Yeah, makes sense. But you must've had some good memories from back then, right? I mean, even if it was a rough area, you had your mates."

Andrew chuckled, though it was tinged with a slight bitterness. "Good memories? Maybe a few. But mostly, it was just… survival, you know? Hanging around with those guys wasn't exactly a choice. I did what I had to do to fit in, to keep my head down."

Simon pressed on, "Like what?"

Andrew sighed, turning to face Simon. "Like… blending in. Doing what they did. They were always looking for trouble–picking on people, getting into fights. It was stupid stuff, but it was safer to be with them than against them."

Simon felt a cold sweat trickle down his spine. Stupid stuff. Was that what Andrew called it? Was that how he justified it? He forced himself to stay calm, to keep the conversation moving without giving away the mounting panic in his chest.

"Did they ever go after… I don't know, specific people? Like, why pick fights with random strangers?"

Andrew hesitated, his brow furrowing slightly. "It was never planned or anything. They just saw someone who looked like an easy target, and that was it. Drunks, homeless people, sometimes couples–anyone they could get a rise out of. I hated it. I hated every second of it."

Simon clenched his fists, fighting back the surge of anger that was rising inside him. Couples. He needed more. He needed to push harder.

"Did they ever… you know, target gay couples?" Simon asked carefully, his voice barely above a whisper.

Andrew's face darkened, and he nodded slowly. "Yeah. They did. Especially them. It made me sick, to be honest. But I couldn't say anything. If I had, they would've known. They would've figured out I was one of the people they were going after."

Simon's breath caught in his throat. His mind flashed back to that night–the jeering voices, the cruel taunts, the way the gang had zeroed in on him and Matthew like hunters closing in on prey. He remembered the way Matthew had tried to shield him, to fight back, and the sickening sound of fists connecting with flesh.

"Did you ever... do anything?" Simon asked, his voice tight.

Andrew shook his head quickly, almost defensively. "No. I just stood there. I kept my mouth shut and tried to stay invisible. I couldn't afford to stand out, Simon. If I didn't blend in, I would've been next. I know it sounds cowardly, but back then... I didn't know what else to do."

Simon's mind was reeling. It was all too close, too familiar. Andrew wasn't confessing, but the more Simon listened, the more the details began to align with his memories of that night. The gang, the beach, the way they'd targeted gay couples–it was all there, hiding in plain sight.

Simon's heart raced, and he had to force himself to breathe, to stay composed. He couldn't confront Andrew yet. He needed more. He needed something definitive.

The days that followed were a constant battle between Simon's growing suspicion and his desire to keep things as normal as possible. He continued to record their conversations, subtly probing for more details while maintaining the façade of a loving relationship. But the tension was building, and Simon could feel it creeping into every aspect of their time together.

He'd lie awake at night, listening to Andrew's steady breathing beside him, and wonder: Was he there? Was Andrew one of the faceless shadows that had attacked them? The thought made Simon's stomach turn, his body tensing with the weight of his unanswered questions.

One evening, as they were walking through the park, Simon decided to push a little harder. "You ever think about the people your mates hurt? Like, do you ever wonder where they are now?"

Andrew looked uncomfortable, shoving his hands in his pockets. "Sometimes, yeah. I don't know. I try not to think about it too much. I hate that I was even there, but it's not like I did anything to them. I just... stood by."

Simon pressed on, his voice tight. "But standing by is still... letting it happen, isn't it?"

Andrew stopped walking, turning to face Simon with a pained expression. "I know, alright? I know I should've done more. But I didn't. And I've had to live with that ever since."

Simon nodded, trying to keep his voice steady despite the turmoil inside him. "Yeah. I get it."

But he didn't. Not really. How could he understand the weight of Andrew's choices when they were still shrouded in mystery? He didn't know whether Andrew had been directly involved or if he had just stood by, watching as Matthew's life was brutally torn from him. The uncertainty was eating away at Simon, slowly but surely.

-

As the days went on, Simon's paranoia only grew. Every word Andrew said, every offhand comment about his past, felt like a potential clue. Simon couldn't help but pick apart every conversation, searching for anything that might confirm his suspicions. But Andrew never gave him the definitive detail he was looking for. There were hints, yes—references to the rough crowd he used to run with, the homophobic attitudes they held, the violence they perpetuated—but nothing concrete. Nothing that Simon could confront him with.

And yet, the tension between them was growing. Simon could feel it like a weight pressing down on his chest. He was living two lives—one in which he was still trying to build something real with Andrew, and another in which he was desperately searching for the truth. It was exhausting, the constant balancing act between nurturing their relationship and probing for incriminating details.

There were moments when Simon would catch himself looking at Andrew with suspicion, his mind racing with the possibility that the man he had grown to care for was also the man who had stood by and let Matthew die. And then there were moments—quiet, tender moments—when Simon would look at Andrew and feel the weight of his affection, the slow bloom of love that had been growing between them despite everything.

But those moments were growing rarer. The more Simon dug into Andrew's past, the more he felt the walls between them solidifying.

He needed more. He needed to be sure. And until then, Simon knew he couldn't rest.

Chapter 16
THE CONFESSION

It had been an ordinary evening–one of those lazy nights spent in Andrew's flat, with the TV flickering softly in the background and half-empty glasses of wine scattered across the coffee table. They had gone out earlier, had a few drinks at a local bar, and by the time they returned to the flat, Andrew was tipsy, his usual careful demeanour softened by alcohol.

Simon, however, wasn't drunk. His mind was sharper than it had been in weeks. He had been preparing for this moment, waiting for the right combination of vulnerability and openness from Andrew to finally get the truth. Tonight, it felt like the moment might come.

They were both slouched on the sofa, Andrew's arm lazily draped across Simon's shoulders, his face flushed from the wine. Simon could feel the weight of Andrew's body pressing against him, the warmth of their closeness. But tonight, it felt different–like Simon was bracing himself for something he couldn't turn back from.

Andrew reached for the vodka bottle on the table, unscrewing the cap with a clumsy twist and pouring himself another drink. Simon watched him silently, his heart pounding. It was time to push harder.

"You know," Simon began carefully, keeping his voice casual, "we've talked a lot about your past... but you've never really told me everything about your mates in Bournemouth."

Andrew laughed, a dry, bitter sound. "There's not much to tell, really. They were idiots. I was an idiot too."

Simon stayed quiet, letting the words settle between them. He knew Andrew was drunk enough to keep talking, but not so drunk that he wouldn't remember this conversation in the morning. It was the perfect balance—just enough alcohol to loosen the truth from his lips.

"Yeah, but you've said you hated what they did, right?" Simon continued, his tone measured. "I mean, the way they went after people... especially gay people. Didn't that bother you?"

Andrew sighed heavily, his head falling back against the sofa. "Yeah. It did. God, it made me sick. But what could I do? I was in the closet, terrified they'd figure me out. If I didn't join in, I'd have been next."

Simon's heart hammered in his chest. Keep going, he told himself. Don't stop now.

"I get that," Simon said, his voice soft, almost sympathetic. "But... you've never really said what you did. Did you just stand by and watch? Or did you...?"

Andrew was quiet for a moment, staring at the ceiling. His eyes were glazed, distant, and Simon could see the cracks forming in the mask Andrew had worn for so long.

"I did things I'm not proud of," Andrew said quietly, his voice thick with regret. "I went along with the violence. I had to. If I didn't, they'd have known. I mean, we weren't just picking on people... we were... we were hurting them."

Simon's stomach twisted, the bile rising in his throat. This was it —the moment he had been dreading, but also the moment he had been waiting for. He needed to know. He needed to hear Andrew say it.

"Hurting them how?" Simon asked, keeping his voice steady despite the fear coiling in his chest.

Andrew closed his eyes, his face contorted with guilt. "We used to... beat them up. Couples. People walking down the street, just minding their own business. We'd chase them, knock them down, kick them... Jesus, I hated it. I hated every second of it."

Simon swallowed hard, forcing himself to ask the question that had been haunting him for weeks. "Did you ever... did you ever go too far? Like... do something you couldn't take back?"

Andrew didn't answer right away. His breathing was heavy, laboured, and Simon could feel the tension in the air thickening, the weight of the confession that was about to come crashing down on both of them.

Finally, Andrew spoke, his voice barely above a whisper. "There was one night... one night where things got out of hand. We'd been drinking, and... there was this couple. Two guys. They were walking by the beach, and the lads went after them. They started beating one of them up, real bad. And I... I don't know what came over me. I... there was a knife."

Simon felt his entire body go cold. His heart seemed to stop in his chest as the words tumbled out of Andrew's mouth. This was it. This was the moment Simon had been preparing for, but nothing could have prepared him for the horror of hearing it confirmed.

"I didn't mean to do it," Andrew continued, his voice breaking. "I swear to God, Simon, I didn't mean to. I was just... I was scared. I didn't want them to turn on me, so I... I stabbed him. This kid. I didn't even know his name. He just... fell, and the lads ran. And I ran too."

Simon's hands trembled as he clenched them into fists, his knuckles turning white. The room seemed to spin around him, Andrew's voice sounding distant, like it was coming from underwater. *This is it. This is the man who killed Matthew.*

"And then what?" Simon asked, his voice tight, barely holding back the fury that was bubbling up inside him.

Andrew's eyes were glazed with tears now, his hands shaking as he ran them through his hair. "I didn't stay to see what happened. I just... I just ran. I didn't even know if he died until I heard it on the news the next day. I never told anyone. I buried it. I buried it so deep that I... I tried to forget. I didn't even know who he was. Just some kid."

Simon felt like he was going to be sick. The air was thick with tension, his chest tight as he struggled to breathe. This was the man he had been falling for. This was the man who had confessed, so casually, to killing the boy Simon had loved more than anything in the world.

"Simon, I–" Andrew started, but Simon cut him off.

Without a word, Simon stood up, his movements stiff and mechanical. He reached for the bottle of vodka that had been sitting on the coffee table, unscrewing the cap and handing it to Andrew. His face was unreadable, his heart hardened against the man who was now sobbing on the couch, broken and ashamed.

Andrew took the bottle with shaking hands, his wide, tear-filled eyes locking onto Simon's as if searching for any hint of forgiveness. "I swear, Simon, I didn't know... I didn't know it was you," he choked out, his voice breaking. "I didn't know our paths had crossed before, not back then, not in Bournemouth, or anywhere. Not until we'd been going out for a while. That's when I put it together, when I realised what I'd done." His breath hitched, guilt flooding his expression. "I've carried that night with me for years. I never wanted to kill anyone. I swear it. But the gang leader–he handed me the knife and told me to man up. I was scared. I didn't know what to do."

Tears streamed down Andrew's face now, his voice desperate, pleading. "When I realised who you were, who Matthew was... it crushed me. I thought maybe if I stayed with you, if I looked after you, I could somehow make up for it. I could give you something to replace what you'd lost. I never wanted this to come out, Simon. I prayed it never would." He paused, his grip on the bottle tightening as he hung his head in shame. "But I knew, deep down, that I couldn't hide from it forever. I'm so sorry. I'm so sorry for everything."

At that, Andrew lifted the bottle to his lips, taking a long, desperate swig, as though the burn of vodka could somehow dull the pain, the shame that clung to every word he had just confessed. His hand trembled as he swallowed, eyes squeezed shut, trying to escape the weight of the truth that had finally come crashing down. Another swig followed, faster this time, his movements frantic, as if drowning himself in alcohol could make the situation disappear.

Simon stood motionless, watching as Andrew gulped down the liquor in a futile attempt to numb the reality of what he had done. Each swig seemed more reckless than the last, as if he could erase not just his confession, but the years of guilt and the irreversible damage of that night. But no amount of vodka could take it back. The truth was out, and nothing—no drink, no apology—could change what Andrew had done.

But Simon didn't respond. He couldn't. Not yet.

He turned away, walking slowly to the bedroom, his mind racing. As soon as he shut the door behind him, Simon's trembling hands reached into his pocket for his phone. His pulse pounded in his ears as he unlocked it, praying the app had recorded every word.

He hit play.

Andrew's voice came through clearly, the words tumbling out like a confession Simon had waited years to hear.

"I had a knife... I stabbed him... I didn't even know his name."

Simon's breath caught in his throat. He had it. He had everything.

He sat down on the edge of the bed, his entire body shaking as the weight of the night settled on him. He had the confession. He had the proof. But the price of knowing the truth was far greater than Simon had ever imagined.

Andrew had killed Matthew.

And now, there was no going back.

Chapter 17
JUSTICE AT LAST

Simon sat on the edge of the bed, his heart pounding in his chest as the minutes stretched on. The faint sounds of Andrew's sobs had faded into silence, and now, the only sound in the flat was the rhythmic ticking of the clock on the wall. The room felt impossibly small, the air thick with the weight of everything that had just transpired. Simon's hands still trembled, the phone heavy in his grip as the recording played on repeat in his mind.

Andrew's confession echoed in his thoughts: "I had a knife... I stabbed him... I didn't even know his name."

The man he had grown to care for–the man who had brought him comfort, who had shown him love again–was the same person who had ripped his world apart all those years ago. Andrew had killed Matthew. The reality of it was suffocating, and Simon couldn't breathe under the weight of that truth. But he knew what he had to do.

Simon slowly stood, his legs weak as if they could barely support him. He glanced back at the living room, where Andrew had passed out, drunk and emotionally spent. The bottle of vodka still rested on the table, the half-empty glass beside it. Andrew lay slumped on the sofa, his body curled in on itself, as though he were trying to hide from his own guilt.

For a brief moment, Simon felt a pang of something—sorrow, regret, maybe even pity. But it was fleeting, quickly replaced by the cold determination that had been driving him since the moment Andrew had confessed. This wasn't just about him anymore. It was about Matthew. About justice.

With a deep breath, Simon picked up his phone and dialled.

The ringing seemed to last forever before a voice finally came through on the other end.

"999, what's your emergency?"

Simon swallowed hard, his voice steady despite the storm inside him. "I need to report a crime. I have evidence... a confession. It's about a murder that happened years ago."

The operator's voice remained calm, professional, but Simon could sense the urgency beneath the surface. "Can you tell me more about the incident, sir?"

Simon closed his eyes, feeling the weight of his words as they left his lips. "The person who killed Matthew Williams... I have a recording. The man who did it... he's here, at my flat. His name is Andrew."

There was a pause, then the operator spoke again. "Officers are on their way, sir. Please stay on the line with me."

Simon gave the operator the address, his heart pounding faster now, the reality of what was about to happen sinking in. He sat down on the bed again, clutching the phone as the seconds ticked by. The steady hum of the operator's voice was a distant murmur, a lifeline that tethered him to the moment, but Simon's thoughts were elsewhere—drifting back to the night Matthew had died, to the brutal attack that had stolen everything from him.

The sound of sirens grew louder, cutting through the quiet of the flat like a sharp blade. Simon's stomach twisted as he heard them approaching, the flashing blue lights spilling through the curtains, casting the room in a cold, eerie glow. He stood, the phone still in his hand, and walked to the window. Outside, he could see the police cars pulling up, officers stepping out, their radios crackling with static as they moved toward the building.

"Sir, officers are at the scene," the operator said, her voice calm. "Can you let them in?"

Simon nodded, though she couldn't see him. "Yeah. I'll go now."

He hung up the phone, feeling a strange numbness settle over him as he walked toward the door. His body felt like it was moving on autopilot, each step deliberate, purposeful. As he reached for the handle, he glanced back at Andrew one last time. The man who had once made him feel safe and loved now lay on the couch, unaware that his life was about to change forever.

Simon opened the door, and the officers were there, their expressions serious but controlled. He stepped aside to let them in, his heart racing as he pointed toward the living room.

"He's in there," Simon whispered. "He confessed... I recorded everything."

One of the officers, a woman with sharp eyes and a calm demeanour, stepped forward. "Thank you, sir. We'll handle it from here."

Simon nodded, retreating to the hallway as the officers moved inside. He stood there, back against the wall, listening as they roused Andrew from his drunken stupor. The murmur of their voices was distant, almost surreal. He heard Andrew mumbling, confused at first, then the sharp intake of breath as he realised what was happening.

"No... no, this can't be happening," Andrew's voice was thick with panic now, slurred from the alcohol but still clear enough for Simon to understand.

Simon felt a strange, detached sense of satisfaction as he heard the clink of handcuffs, the rustling of movement as the officers led Andrew out of the flat. He didn't move, didn't look up, but he could feel the weight of Andrew's gaze as he was led past the hallway, the heavy footsteps of the officers echoing through the quiet space.

"Simon?" Andrew's voice cracked, desperate. "Simon, please—"

But Simon didn't respond. He couldn't. He stood there, frozen, as Andrew was led out of the flat and down the stairs. The door clicked shut, and the flat fell into silence once again, broken only by the faint murmur of voices outside.

Simon finally pushed himself off the wall, moving slowly to the window. He watched from a distance as the officers guided Andrew toward the waiting police car. Andrew's face was pale, his eyes wide with fear and disbelief. He looked broken, a far cry from the confident, carefree man Simon had once known.

As the officers placed Andrew in the back of the car, Simon felt an overwhelming mix of emotions—triumph, sorrow, and a deep, aching sense of loss. He had finally done it. Justice for Matthew was being served. The man who had stolen Matthew's life, who had destroyed Simon's world, was being taken away in handcuffs. The man who had also been Simon's lover, someone he had let into his life, was now just another criminal awaiting his fate.

But as much as Simon had wanted this moment, it didn't feel like a victory. The emptiness inside him remained, the gaping hole that Matthew's death had left behind still raw and aching. There was no joy in this, no relief. Just the quiet, crushing finality of knowing that justice had come at the cost of his own heart.

Andrew had been the person who had helped Simon find a piece of himself again, but in the end, he was also the person who had taken everything away.

The police car pulled away from the curb, disappearing into the distance, and Simon stood there, staring out at the darkened street. He had done what he needed to do. Matthew would finally have justice. But Simon was left standing alone, his heart heavy with the weight of all that had been lost.

Chapter 18
THE ROAD AHEAD

The months that followed Andrew's arrest had been a blur. There were days when Simon felt like he was finally free, able to breathe without the suffocating weight of his past pressing down on him. But there were also moments when the guilt and grief threatened to pull him under again, like the tides that never stopped crashing against the shore. It had been a long, painful journey, and even now, with Andrew behind bars, the scars of what had happened remained.

Andrew had been found guilty of manslaughter. The trial had been agonising–reliving every brutal detail of that night, watching Andrew in the dock, seeing the face of a man Simon had once cared for now twisted with shame and regret. But Andrew's confession, the recording Simon had captured, left little room for doubt. He had been sentenced to twelve years in prison. Twelve years for the life that had been taken.

It didn't feel like enough. But then again, Simon wasn't sure any sentence could ever feel like enough.

As the months passed, Simon found himself reflecting more and more on the weight of everything that had happened. He thought about Matthew often—his laugh, the way his smile could light up a room, the quiet moments they'd shared by the sea. Matthew had been everything to him, and for years, Simon had been consumed by the grief of losing him. But now, with Andrew in prison and the truth finally out in the open, Simon realised he was no longer haunted by that night in the same way.

The closure he had been searching for wasn't the sense of triumph he had imagined. It was quieter, subtler. It wasn't about revenge or justice, not entirely. It was about letting go—of the pain, the guilt, the unanswered questions. It was about allowing himself to heal.

He wasn't sure where life would take him next. He hadn't planned that far ahead. For so long, his life had been focused on getting to this point, on finding closure, on making sure that Matthew's death wasn't forgotten. But now that it was over, Simon felt a strange sense of freedom, as if the future was finally his to shape again.

The weather that day was stormy, the sky above a moody grey, with dark clouds swirling on the horizon. Simon walked along the coast, the cold sea air whipping through his hair, the sound of the crashing waves a steady rhythm that mirrored his thoughts. The path was quiet, the usual crowds deterred by the looming storm, and Simon welcomed the solitude.

Each step felt lighter than the last. He wasn't the same person he had been all those years ago, when Matthew's death had shattered his world. He had grown, changed, and though the pain of that loss would always be with him, it no longer defined him. He was more than his past, more than the boy who had lost the love of his life to violence. He had survived, and now, he was ready to move forward.

As he walked, his thoughts drifted to the future—what it might hold, where it might take him. He hadn't thought much about relationships, not since Andrew, but there was a quiet hope now. Hope that one day, he might be ready to open himself up to love again. Maybe not today, maybe not tomorrow, but someday.

The wind picked up, and Simon pulled his jacket tighter around him, his eyes scanning the coastline ahead. The waves crashed violently against the rocks, the stormy sea a perfect reflection of the chaos and peace that had shaped his life over the past few years. Pain and promise, mingling together, just like the ocean before him.

He stopped at a small kiosk that stood on the edge of the promenade, its bright colours standing out against the grey day. The sign above it advertised ice cream, and despite the cold, Simon found himself drawn to it. The idea of a 99 ice cream felt oddly nostalgic, a small comfort on a day like today.

He approached the counter, where a young man stood, wearing a food safety hair net and a red apron over a tight-fitting T-shirt. He looked up as Simon approached, a friendly smile spreading across his face.

"Bit stormy for an ice cream, eh?" the man said, his tone light, as though the weather were nothing more than a minor inconvenience.

Simon smiled back, feeling the tension in his chest ease a little. "Yeah, but I figured, why not?"

The man chuckled as he reached for the soft-serve machine. "Fair enough. Maybe the weather'll clear up before the pride event in a couple of days. Fingers crossed for some sun."

Simon raised an eyebrow, intrigued. "Pride? Here?"

"Yeah," the man said, glancing over his shoulder as the ice cream swirled into the cone. "They're doing a big event. Parade, music, all the usual stuff. You should come down. It's always a good time."

"Maybe I will," Simon said, his smile growing.

The man finished the ice cream and handed it to Simon, and to his surprise, it had not one but two flakes nestled in the swirl of soft-serve.

"Two flakes," the man said with a wink. "On the house."

Simon chuckled, taking the cone from him. "Thanks. I appreciate it."

"No problem," the man said with an easy smile. "Enjoy your walk."

Simon nodded, feeling lighter as he turned away from the kiosk. He resumed his stroll along the coast, the ice cream in hand, the wind still sharp but somehow less biting now. The storm clouds above threatened rain, but Simon didn't care. The cold air felt fresh, clean, like a new beginning.

As he walked, Simon took a deep breath, the salt in the air filling his lungs. The road ahead was uncertain, but for the first time in a long time, he felt ready for whatever it might bring. He had survived the worst of it, had faced his darkest fears, and now, he was free. Free to live, to move forward, to find happiness again.

He licked the ice cream, the taste sweet and familiar, and continued his walk, alone but at peace.

Printed in Great Britain
by Amazon